THIS IS YOUR **PASSBOOK**® FOR ...

STEAMFITTER'S APPRENTICE APTITUDE TEST

NATIONAL LEARNING CORPORATION®
passbooks.com

PASSBOOK® SERIES

THE *PASSBOOK® SERIES* has been created to prepare applicants and candidates for the ultimate academic battlefield – the examination room.

At some time in our lives, each and every one of us may be required to take an examination – for validation, matriculation, admission, qualification, registration, certification, or licensure.

Based on the assumption that every applicant or candidate has met the basic formal educational standards, has taken the required number of courses, and read the necessary texts, the *PASSBOOK® SERIES* furnishes the one special preparation which may assure passing with confidence, instead of failing with insecurity. Examination questions – together with answers – are furnished as the basic vehicle for study so that the mysteries of the examination and its compounding difficulties may be eliminated or diminished by a sure method.

This book is meant to help you pass your examination provided that you qualify and are serious in your objective.

The entire field is reviewed through the huge store of content information which is succinctly presented through a provocative and challenging approach – the question-and-answer method.

A climate of success is established by furnishing the correct answers at the end of each test.

You soon learn to recognize types of questions, forms of questions, and patterns of questioning. You may even begin to anticipate expected outcomes.

You perceive that many questions are repeated or adapted so that you can gain acute insights, which may enable you to score many sure points.

You learn how to confront new questions, or types of questions, and to attack them confidently and work out the correct answers.

You note objectives and emphases, and recognize pitfalls and dangers, so that you may make positive educational adjustments.

Moreover, you are kept fully informed in relation to new concepts, methods, practices, and directions in the field.

You discover that you arre actually taking the examination all the time: you are preparing for the examination by "taking" an examination, not by reading extraneous and/or supererogatory textbooks.

In short, this PASSBOOK®, used directedly, should be an important factor in helping you to pass your test.

STEAMFITTER'S APPRENTICE APTITUDE TEST

DESCRIPTION

To gain admittance into the Steamfitter's Apprentice Recruitment Program, candidates must pass an aptitude test designed to measure skills necessary to become steamfitters.

SCOPE OF THE EXAMINATION

The written test will cover knowledge, skills and/or abilities in such areas as:

1. Mechanical aptitude;
2. Tool recognition and use;
3. Reading comprehension; and
4. Arithmetical reasoning.

HOW TO TAKE A TEST

I. YOU MUST PASS AN EXAMINATION

A. WHAT EVERY CANDIDATE SHOULD KNOW

Examination applicants often ask us for help in preparing for the written test. What can I study in advance? What kinds of questions will be asked? How will the test be given? How will the papers be graded?

As an applicant for a civil service examination, you may be wondering about some of these things. Our purpose here is to suggest effective methods of advance study and to describe civil service examinations.

Your chances for success on this examination can be increased if you know how to prepare. Those "pre-examination jitters" can be reduced if you know what to expect. You can even experience an adventure in good citizenship if you know why civil service exams are given.

B. WHY ARE CIVIL SERVICE EXAMINATIONS GIVEN?

Civil service examinations are important to you in two ways. As a citizen, you want public jobs filled by employees who know how to do their work. As a job seeker, you want a fair chance to compete for that job on an equal footing with other candidates. The best-known means of accomplishing this two-fold goal is the competitive examination.

Exams are widely publicized throughout the nation. They may be administered for jobs in federal, state, city, municipal, town or village governments or agencies.

Any citizen may apply, with some limitations, such as the age or residence of applicants. Your experience and education may be reviewed to see whether you meet the requirements for the particular examination. When these requirements exist, they are reasonable and applied consistently to all applicants. Thus, a competitive examination may cause you some uneasiness now, but it is your privilege and safeguard.

C. HOW ARE CIVIL SERVICE EXAMS DEVELOPED?

Examinations are carefully written by trained technicians who are specialists in the field known as "psychological measurement," in consultation with recognized authorities in the field of work that the test will cover. These experts recommend the subject matter areas or skills to be tested; only those knowledges or skills important to your success on the job are included. The most reliable books and source materials available are used as references. Together, the experts and technicians judge the difficulty level of the questions.

Test technicians know how to phrase questions so that the problem is clearly stated. Their ethics do not permit "trick" or "catch" questions. Questions may have been tried out on sample groups, or subjected to statistical analysis, to determine their usefulness.

Written tests are often used in combination with performance tests, ratings of training and experience, and oral interviews. All of these measures combine to form the best-known means of finding the right person for the right job.

II. HOW TO PASS THE WRITTEN TEST

A. NATURE OF THE EXAMINATION

To prepare intelligently for civil service examinations, you should know how they differ from school examinations you have taken. In school you were assigned certain definite pages to read or subjects to cover. The examination questions were quite detailed and usually emphasized memory. Civil service exams, on the other hand, try to discover your present ability to perform the duties of a position, plus your potentiality to learn these duties. In other words, a civil service exam attempts to predict how successful you will be. Questions cover such a broad area that they cannot be as minute and detailed as school exam questions.

In the public service similar kinds of work, or positions, are grouped together in one "class." This process is known as *position-classification*. All the positions in a class are paid according to the salary range for that class. One class title covers all of these positions, and they are all tested by the same examination.

B. FOUR BASIC STEPS

1) Study the announcement

How, then, can you know what subjects to study? Our best answer is: "Learn as much as possible about the class of positions for which you've applied." The exam will test the knowledge, skills and abilities needed to do the work.

Your most valuable source of information about the position you want is the official exam announcement. This announcement lists the training and experience qualifications. Check these standards and apply only if you come reasonably close to meeting them.

The brief description of the position in the examination announcement offers some clues to the subjects which will be tested. Think about the job itself. Review the duties in your mind. Can you perform them, or are there some in which you are rusty? Fill in the blank spots in your preparation.

Many jurisdictions preview the written test in the exam announcement by including a section called "Knowledge and Abilities Required," "Scope of the Examination," or some similar heading. Here you will find out specifically what fields will be tested.

2) Review your own background

Once you learn in general what the position is all about, and what you need to know to do the work, ask yourself which subjects you already know fairly well and which need improvement. You may wonder whether to concentrate on improving your strong areas or on building some background in your fields of weakness. When the announcement has specified "some knowledge" or "considerable knowledge," or has used adjectives like "beginning principles of..." or "advanced ... methods," you can get a clue as to the number and difficulty of questions to be asked in any given field. More questions, and hence broader coverage, would be included for those subjects which are more important in the work. Now weigh your strengths and weaknesses against the job requirements and prepare accordingly.

3) Determine the level of the position

Another way to tell how intensively you should prepare is to understand the level of the job for which you are applying. Is it the entering level? In other words, is this the position in which beginners in a field of work are hired? Or is it an intermediate or advanced level? Sometimes this is indicated by such words as "Junior" or "Senior" in the class title. Other jurisdictions use Roman numerals to designate the level – Clerk I, Clerk II, for example. The word "Supervisor" sometimes appears in the title. If the level is not indicated by the title, check the description of duties. Will you be working under very close supervision, or will you have responsibility for independent decisions in this work?

4) Choose appropriate study materials

Now that you know the subjects to be examined and the relative amount of each subject to be covered, you can choose suitable study materials. For beginning level jobs, or even advanced ones, if you have a pronounced weakness in some aspect of your training, read a modern, standard textbook in that field. Be sure it is up to date and has general coverage. Such books are normally available at your library, and the librarian will be glad to help you locate one. For entry-level positions, questions of appropriate difficulty are chosen – neither highly advanced questions, nor those too simple. Such questions require careful thought but not advanced training.

If the position for which you are applying is technical or advanced, you will read more advanced, specialized material. If you are already familiar with the basic principles of your field, elementary textbooks would waste your time. Concentrate on advanced textbooks and technical periodicals. Think through the concepts and review difficult problems in your field.

These are all general sources. You can get more ideas on your own initiative, following these leads. For example, training manuals and publications of the government agency which employs workers in your field can be useful, particularly for technical and professional positions. A letter or visit to the government department involved may result in more specific study suggestions, and certainly will provide you with a more definite idea of the exact nature of the position you are seeking.

III. KINDS OF TESTS

Tests are used for purposes other than measuring knowledge and ability to perform specified duties. For some positions, it is equally important to test ability to make adjustments to new situations or to profit from training. In others, basic mental abilities not dependent on information are essential. Questions which test these things may not appear as pertinent to the duties of the position as those which test for knowledge and information. Yet they are often highly important parts of a fair examination. For very general questions, it is almost impossible to help you direct your study efforts. What we can do is to point out some of the more common of these general abilities needed in public service positions and describe some typical questions.

1) General information

Broad, general information has been found useful for predicting job success in some kinds of work. This is tested in a variety of ways, from vocabulary lists to questions about current events. Basic background in some field of work, such as sociology or economics, may be sampled in a group of questions. Often these are principles which have become familiar to most persons through exposure rather than through formal training. It is difficult to advise you how to study for these questions; being alert to the world around you is our best suggestion.

2) Verbal ability

An example of an ability needed in many positions is verbal or language ability. Verbal ability is, in brief, the ability to use and understand words. Vocabulary and grammar tests are typical measures of this ability. Reading comprehension or paragraph interpretation questions are common in many kinds of civil service tests. You are given a paragraph of written material and asked to find its central meaning.

3) Numerical ability

Number skills can be tested by the familiar arithmetic problem, by checking paired lists of numbers to see which are alike and which are different, or by interpreting charts and graphs. In the latter test, a graph may be printed in the test booklet which you are asked to use as the basis for answering questions.

4) Observation

A popular test for law-enforcement positions is the observation test. A picture is shown to you for several minutes, then taken away. Questions about the picture test your ability to observe both details and larger elements.

5) Following directions

In many positions in the public service, the employee must be able to carry out written instructions dependably and accurately. You may be given a chart with several columns, each column listing a variety of information. The questions require you to carry out directions involving the information given in the chart.

6) Skills and aptitudes

Performance tests effectively measure some manual skills and aptitudes. When the skill is one in which you are trained, such as typing or shorthand, you can practice. These tests are often very much like those given in business school or high school courses. For many of the other skills and aptitudes, however, no short-time preparation can be made. Skills and abilities natural to you or that you have developed throughout your lifetime are being tested.

Many of the general questions just described provide all the data needed to answer the questions and ask you to use your reasoning ability to find the answers. Your best preparation for these tests, as well as for tests of facts and ideas, is to be at your physical and mental best. You, no doubt, have your own methods of getting into an exam-taking mood and keeping "in shape." The next section lists some ideas on this subject.

IV. KINDS OF QUESTIONS

Only rarely is the "essay" question, which you answer in narrative form, used in civil service tests. Civil service tests are usually of the short-answer type. Full instructions for answering these questions will be given to you at the examination. But in case this is your first experience with short-answer questions and separate answer sheets, here is what you need to know:

1) Multiple-choice Questions

Most popular of the short-answer questions is the "multiple choice" or "best answer" question. It can be used, for example, to test for factual knowledge, ability to solve problems or judgment in meeting situations found at work.

A multiple-choice question is normally one of three types—

- It can begin with an incomplete statement followed by several possible endings. You are to find the one ending which *best* completes the statement, although some of the others may not be entirely wrong.
- It can also be a complete statement in the form of a question which is answered by choosing one of the statements listed.
- It can be in the form of a problem – again you select the best answer.

Here is an example of a multiple-choice question with a discussion which should give you some clues as to the method for choosing the right answer:

When an employee has a complaint about his assignment, the action which will *best* help him overcome his difficulty is to
- A. discuss his difficulty with his coworkers
- B. take the problem to the head of the organization
- C. take the problem to the person who gave him the assignment
- D. say nothing to anyone about his complaint

In answering this question, you should study each of the choices to find which is best. Consider choice "A" – Certainly an employee may discuss his complaint with fellow employees, but no change or improvement can result, and the complaint remains unresolved. Choice "B" is a poor choice since the head of the organization probably does not know what assignment you have been given, and taking your problem to him is known as "going over the head" of the supervisor. The supervisor, or person who made the assignment, is the person who can clarify it or correct any injustice. Choice "C" is, therefore, correct. To say nothing, as in choice "D," is unwise. Supervisors have and interest in knowing the problems employees are facing, and the employee is seeking a solution to his problem.

2) True/False Questions

The "true/false" or "right/wrong" form of question is sometimes used. Here a complete statement is given. Your job is to decide whether the statement is right or wrong.

SAMPLE: A roaming cell-phone call to a nearby city costs less than a non-roaming call to a distant city.

This statement is wrong, or false, since roaming calls are more expensive.

This is not a complete list of all possible question forms, although most of the others are variations of these common types. You will always get complete directions for answering questions. Be sure you understand *how* to mark your answers – ask questions until you do.

V. RECORDING YOUR ANSWERS

Computer terminals are used more and more today for many different kinds of exams.

For an examination with very few applicants, you may be told to record your answers in the test booklet itself. Separate answer sheets are much more common. If this separate answer sheet is to be scored by machine – and this is often the case – it is highly important that you mark your answers correctly in order to get credit.

An electronic scoring machine is often used in civil service offices because of the speed with which papers can be scored. Machine-scored answer sheets must be marked with a pencil, which will be given to you. This pencil has a high graphite content which responds to the electronic scoring machine. As a matter of fact, stray dots may register as answers, so do not let your pencil rest on the answer sheet while you are pondering the correct answer. Also, if your pencil lead breaks or is otherwise defective, ask for another.

Since the answer sheet will be dropped in a slot in the scoring machine, be careful not to bend the corners or get the paper crumpled.

The answer sheet normally has five vertical columns of numbers, with 30 numbers to a column. These numbers correspond to the question numbers in your test booklet. After each number, going across the page are four or five pairs of dotted lines. These short dotted lines have small letters or numbers above them. The first two pairs may also have a "T" or "F" above the letters. This indicates that the first two pairs only are to be used if the questions are of the true-false type. If the questions are multiple choice, disregard the "T" and "F" and pay attention only to the small letters or numbers.

Answer your questions in the manner of the sample that follows:

32. The largest city in the United States is
    A. Washington, D.C.
    B. New York City
    C. Chicago
    D. Detroit
    E. San Francisco

1) Choose the answer you think is best. (New York City is the largest, so "B" is correct.)
2) Find the row of dotted lines numbered the same as the question you are answering. (Find row number 32)
3) Find the pair of dotted lines corresponding to the answer. (Find the pair of lines under the mark "B.")
4) Make a solid black mark between the dotted lines.

VI. BEFORE THE TEST

Common sense will help you find procedures to follow to get ready for an examination. Too many of us, however, overlook these sensible measures. Indeed, nervousness and fatigue have been found to be the most serious reasons why applicants fail to do their best on civil service tests. Here is a list of reminders:

- Begin your preparation early – Don't wait until the last minute to go scurrying around for books and materials or to find out what the position is all about.
- Prepare continuously – An hour a night for a week is better than an all-night cram session. This has been definitely established. What is more, a night a week for a month will return better dividends than crowding your study into a shorter period of time.
- Locate the place of the exam – You have been sent a notice telling you when and where to report for the examination. If the location is in a different town or otherwise unfamiliar to you, it would be well to inquire the best route and learn something about the building.
- Relax the night before the test – Allow your mind to rest. Do not study at all that night. Plan some mild recreation or diversion; then go to bed early and get a good night's sleep.
- Get up early enough to make a leisurely trip to the place for the test – This way unforeseen events, traffic snarls, unfamiliar buildings, etc. will not upset you.
- Dress comfortably – A written test is not a fashion show. You will be known by number and not by name, so wear something comfortable.
- Leave excess paraphernalia at home – Shopping bags and odd bundles will get in your way. You need bring only the items mentioned in the official notice you received; usually everything you need is provided. Do not bring reference books to the exam. They will only confuse those last minutes and be taken away from you when in the test room.
- Arrive somewhat ahead of time – If because of transportation schedules you must get there very early, bring a newspaper or magazine to take your mind off yourself while waiting.
- Locate the examination room – When you have found the proper room, you will be directed to the seat or part of the room where you will sit. Sometimes you are given a sheet of instructions to read while you are waiting. Do not fill out any forms until you are told to do so; just read them and be prepared.
- Relax and prepare to listen to the instructions
- If you have any physical problem that may keep you from doing your best, be sure to tell the test administrator. If you are sick or in poor health, you really cannot do your best on the exam. You can come back and take the test some other time.

VII. AT THE TEST

The day of the test is here and you have the test booklet in your hand. The temptation to get going is very strong. Caution! There is more to success than knowing the right answers. You must know how to identify your papers and understand variations in the type of short-answer question used in this particular examination. Follow these suggestions for maximum results from your efforts:

1) Cooperate with the monitor

The test administrator has a duty to create a situation in which you can be as much at ease as possible. He will give instructions, tell you when to begin, check to see that you are marking your answer sheet correctly, and so on. He is not there to guard you, although he will see that your competitors do not take unfair advantage. He wants to help you do your best.

2) Listen to all instructions

Don't jump the gun! Wait until you understand all directions. In most civil service tests you get more time than you need to answer the questions. So don't be in a hurry. Read each word of instructions until you clearly understand the meaning. Study the examples, listen to all announcements and follow directions. Ask questions if you do not understand what to do.

3) Identify your papers

Civil service exams are usually identified by number only. You will be assigned a number; you must not put your name on your test papers. Be sure to copy your number correctly. Since more than one exam may be given, copy your exact examination title.

4) Plan your time

Unless you are told that a test is a "speed" or "rate of work" test, speed itself is usually not important. Time enough to answer all the questions will be provided, but this does not mean that you have all day. An overall time limit has been set. Divide the total time (in minutes) by the number of questions to determine the approximate time you have for each question.

5) Do not linger over difficult questions

If you come across a difficult question, mark it with a paper clip (useful to have along) and come back to it when you have been through the booklet. One caution if you do this – be sure to skip a number on your answer sheet as well. Check often to be sure that you have not lost your place and that you are marking in the row numbered the same as the question you are answering.

6) Read the questions

Be sure you know what the question asks! Many capable people are unsuccessful because they failed to *read* the questions correctly.

7) Answer all questions

Unless you have been instructed that a penalty will be deducted for incorrect answers, it is better to guess than to omit a question.

8) Speed tests

It is often better NOT to guess on speed tests. It has been found that on timed tests people are tempted to spend the last few seconds before time is called in marking answers at random – without even reading them – in the hope of picking up a few extra points. To discourage this practice, the instructions may warn you that your score will be "corrected" for guessing. That is, a penalty will be applied. The incorrect answers will be deducted from the correct ones, or some other penalty formula will be used.

9) Review your answers

If you finish before time is called, go back to the questions you guessed or omitted to give them further thought. Review other answers if you have time.

10) Return your test materials

If you are ready to leave before others have finished or time is called, take ALL your materials to the monitor and leave quietly. Never take any test material with you. The monitor can discover whose papers are not complete, and taking a test booklet may be grounds for disqualification.

VIII. EXAMINATION TECHNIQUES

1) Read the general instructions carefully. These are usually printed on the first page of the exam booklet. As a rule, these instructions refer to the timing of the examination; the fact that you should not start work until the signal and must stop work at a signal, etc. If there are any *special* instructions, such as a choice of questions to be answered, make sure that you note this instruction carefully.

2) When you are ready to start work on the examination, that is as soon as the signal has been given, read the instructions to each question booklet, underline any key words or phrases, such as *least, best, outline, describe* and the like. In this way you will tend to answer as requested rather than discover on reviewing your paper that you *listed without describing*, that you selected the *worst* choice rather than the *best* choice, etc.

3) If the examination is of the objective or multiple-choice type – that is, each question will also give a series of possible answers: A, B, C or D, and you are called upon to select the best answer and write the letter next to that answer on your answer paper – it is advisable to start answering each question in turn. There may be anywhere from 50 to 100 such questions in the three or four hours allotted and you can see how much time would be taken if you read through all the questions before beginning to answer any. Furthermore, if you come across a question or group of questions which you know would be difficult to answer, it would undoubtedly affect your handling of all the other questions.

4) If the examination is of the essay type and contains but a few questions, it is a moot point as to whether you should read all the questions before starting to answer any one. Of course, if you are given a choice – say five out of seven and the like – then it is essential to read all the questions so you can eliminate the two that are most difficult. If, however, you are asked to answer all the questions, there may be danger in trying to answer the easiest one first because you may find that you will spend too much time on it. The best technique is to answer the first question, then proceed to the second, etc.

5) Time your answers. Before the exam begins, write down the time it started, then add the time allowed for the examination and write down the time it must be completed, then divide the time available somewhat as follows:

- If 3-1/2 hours are allowed, that would be 210 minutes. If you have 80 objective-type questions, that would be an average of 2-1/2 minutes per question. Allow yourself no more than 2 minutes per question, or a total of 160 minutes, which will permit about 50 minutes to review.
- If for the time allotment of 210 minutes there are 7 essay questions to answer, that would average about 30 minutes a question. Give yourself only 25 minutes per question so that you have about 35 minutes to review.

6) The most important instruction is to *read each question* and make sure you know what is wanted. The second most important instruction is to *time yourself properly* so that you answer every question. The third most important instruction is to *answer every question*. Guess if you have to but include something for each question. Remember that you will receive no credit for a blank and will probably receive some credit if you write something in answer to an essay question. If you guess a letter – say "B" for a multiple-choice question – you may have guessed right. If you leave a blank as an answer to a multiple-choice question, the examiners may respect your feelings but it will not add a point to your score. Some exams may penalize you for wrong answers, so in such cases *only*, you may not want to guess unless you have some basis for your answer.

7) Suggestions
   a. Objective-type questions
      1. Examine the question booklet for proper sequence of pages and questions
      2. Read all instructions carefully
      3. Skip any question which seems too difficult; return to it after all other questions have been answered
      4. Apportion your time properly; do not spend too much time on any single question or group of questions
      5. Note and underline key words – *all, most, fewest, least, best, worst, same, opposite*, etc.
      6. Pay particular attention to negatives
      7. Note unusual option, e.g., unduly long, short, complex, different or similar in content to the body of the question
      8. Observe the use of "hedging" words – *probably, may, most likely,* etc.
      9. Make sure that your answer is put next to the same number as the question
      10. Do not second-guess unless you have good reason to believe the second answer is definitely more correct
      11. Cross out original answer if you decide another answer is more accurate; do not erase until you are ready to hand your paper in
      12. Answer all questions; guess unless instructed otherwise
      13. Leave time for review

   b. Essay questions
      1. Read each question carefully
      2. Determine exactly what is wanted. Underline key words or phrases.
      3. Decide on outline or paragraph answer

4. Include many different points and elements unless asked to develop any one or two points or elements
5. Show impartiality by giving pros and cons unless directed to select one side only
6. Make and write down any assumptions you find necessary to answer the questions
7. Watch your English, grammar, punctuation and choice of words
8. Time your answers; don't crowd material

8) Answering the essay question

Most essay questions can be answered by framing the specific response around several key words or ideas. Here are a few such key words or ideas:

M's: manpower, materials, methods, money, management
P's: purpose, program, policy, plan, procedure, practice, problems, pitfalls, personnel, public relations
  a. Six basic steps in handling problems:
     1. Preliminary plan and background development
     2. Collect information, data and facts
     3. Analyze and interpret information, data and facts
     4. Analyze and develop solutions as well as make recommendations
     5. Prepare report and sell recommendations
     6. Install recommendations and follow up effectiveness

  b. Pitfalls to avoid
     1. *Taking things for granted* – A statement of the situation does not necessarily imply that each of the elements is necessarily true; for example, a complaint may be invalid and biased so that all that can be taken for granted is that a complaint has been registered
     2. *Considering only one side of a situation* – Wherever possible, indicate several alternatives and then point out the reasons you selected the best one
     3. *Failing to indicate follow up* – Whenever your answer indicates action on your part, make certain that you will take proper follow-up action to see how successful your recommendations, procedures or actions turn out to be
     4. *Taking too long in answering any single question* – Remember to time your answers properly

IX. AFTER THE TEST

Scoring procedures differ in detail among civil service jurisdictions although the general principles are the same. Whether the papers are hand-scored or graded by machine we have described, they are nearly always graded by number. That is, the person who marks the paper knows only the number – never the name – of the applicant. Not until all the papers have been graded will they be matched with names. If other tests, such as training and experience or oral interview ratings have been given, scores will be combined. Different parts of the examination usually have different weights. For example, the written test might count 60 percent of the final grade, and a rating of training and experience 40 percent. In many jurisdictions, veterans will have a certain number of points added to their grades.

After the final grade has been determined, the names are placed in grade order and an eligible list is established. There are various methods for resolving ties between those who get the same final grade – probably the most common is to place first the name of the person whose application was received first. Job offers are made from the eligible list in the order the names appear on it. You will be notified of your grade and your rank as soon as all these computations have been made. This will be done as rapidly as possible.

People who are found to meet the requirements in the announcement are called "eligibles." Their names are put on a list of eligible candidates. An eligible's chances of getting a job depend on how high he stands on this list and how fast agencies are filling jobs from the list.

When a job is to be filled from a list of eligibles, the agency asks for the names of people on the list of eligibles for that job. When the civil service commission receives this request, it sends to the agency the names of the three people highest on this list. Or, if the job to be filled has specialized requirements, the office sends the agency the names of the top three persons who meet these requirements from the general list.

The appointing officer makes a choice from among the three people whose names were sent to him. If the selected person accepts the appointment, the names of the others are put back on the list to be considered for future openings.

That is the rule in hiring from all kinds of eligible lists, whether they are for typist, carpenter, chemist, or something else. For every vacancy, the appointing officer has his choice of any one of the top three eligibles on the list. This explains why the person whose name is on top of the list sometimes does not get an appointment when some of the persons lower on the list do. If the appointing officer chooses the second or third eligible, the No. 1 eligible does not get a job at once, but stays on the list until he is appointed or the list is terminated.

X. HOW TO PASS THE INTERVIEW TEST

The examination for which you applied requires an oral interview test. You have already taken the written test and you are now being called for the interview test – the final part of the formal examination.

You may think that it is not possible to prepare for an interview test and that there are no procedures to follow during an interview. Our purpose is to point out some things you can do in advance that will help you and some good rules to follow and pitfalls to avoid while you are being interviewed.

What is an interview supposed to test?

The written examination is designed to test the technical knowledge and competence of the candidate; the oral is designed to evaluate intangible qualities, not readily measured otherwise, and to establish a list showing the relative fitness of each candidate – as measured against his competitors – for the position sought. Scoring is not on the basis of "right" and "wrong," but on a sliding scale of values ranging from "not passable" to "outstanding." As a matter of fact, it is possible to achieve a relatively low score without a single "incorrect" answer because of evident weakness in the qualities being measured.

Occasionally, an examination may consist entirely of an oral test – either an individual or a group oral. In such cases, information is sought concerning the technical knowledges and abilities of the candidate, since there has been no written examination for this purpose. More commonly, however, an oral test is used to supplement a written examination.

Who conducts interviews?

The composition of oral boards varies among different jurisdictions. In nearly all, a representative of the personnel department serves as chairman. One of the members of the board may be a representative of the department in which the candidate would work. In some cases, "outside experts" are used, and, frequently, a businessman or some other representative of the general public is asked to serve. Labor and management or other special groups may be represented. The aim is to secure the services of experts in the appropriate field.

However the board is composed, it is a good idea (and not at all improper or unethical) to ascertain in advance of the interview who the members are and what groups they represent. When you are introduced to them, you will have some idea of their backgrounds and interests, and at least you will not stutter and stammer over their names.

What should be done before the interview?

While knowledge about the board members is useful and takes some of the surprise element out of the interview, there is other preparation which is more substantive. It *is* possible to prepare for an oral interview – in several ways:

1) Keep a copy of your application and review it carefully before the interview

This may be the only document before the oral board, and the starting point of the interview. Know what education and experience you have listed there, and the sequence and dates of all of it. Sometimes the board will ask you to review the highlights of your experience for them; you should not have to hem and haw doing it.

2) Study the class specification and the examination announcement

Usually, the oral board has one or both of these to guide them. The qualities, characteristics or knowledges required by the position sought are stated in these documents. They offer valuable clues as to the nature of the oral interview. For example, if the job involves supervisory responsibilities, the announcement will usually indicate that knowledge of modern supervisory methods and the qualifications of the candidate as a supervisor will be tested. If so, you can expect such questions, frequently in the form of a hypothetical situation which you are expected to solve. NEVER go into an oral without knowledge of the duties and responsibilities of the job you seek.

3) Think through each qualification required

Try to visualize the kind of questions you would ask if you were a board member. How well could you answer them? Try especially to appraise your own knowledge and background in each area, *measured against the job sought*, and identify any areas in which you are weak. Be critical and realistic – do not flatter yourself.

4) Do some general reading in areas in which you feel you may be weak

For example, if the job involves supervision and your past experience has NOT, some general reading in supervisory methods and practices, particularly in the field of human relations, might be useful. Do NOT study agency procedures or detailed manuals. The oral board will be testing your understanding and capacity, not your memory.

5) Get a good night's sleep and watch your general health and mental attitude

You will want a clear head at the interview. Take care of a cold or any other minor ailment, and of course, no hangovers.

What should be done on the day of the interview?

Now comes the day of the interview itself. Give yourself plenty of time to get there. Plan to arrive somewhat ahead of the scheduled time, particularly if your appointment is in the fore part of the day. If a previous candidate fails to appear, the board might be ready for you a bit early. By early afternoon an oral board is almost invariably behind schedule if there are many candidates, and you may have to wait. Take along a book or magazine to read, or your application to review, but leave any extraneous material in the waiting room when you go in for your interview. In any event, relax and compose yourself.

The matter of dress is important. The board is forming impressions about you – from your experience, your manners, your attitude, and your appearance. Give your personal appearance careful attention. Dress your best, but not your flashiest. Choose conservative, appropriate clothing, and be sure it is immaculate. This is a business interview, and your appearance should indicate that you regard it as such. Besides, being well groomed and properly dressed will help boost your confidence.

Sooner or later, someone will call your name and escort you into the interview room. *This is it.* From here on you are on your own. It is too late for any more preparation. But remember, you asked for this opportunity to prove your fitness, and you are here because your request was granted.

What happens when you go in?

The usual sequence of events will be as follows: The clerk (who is often the board stenographer) will introduce you to the chairman of the oral board, who will introduce you to the other members of the board. Acknowledge the introductions before you sit down. Do not be surprised if you find a microphone facing you or a stenotypist sitting by. Oral interviews are usually recorded in the event of an appeal or other review.

Usually the chairman of the board will open the interview by reviewing the highlights of your education and work experience from your application – primarily for the benefit of the other members of the board, as well as to get the material into the record. Do not interrupt or comment unless there is an error or significant misinterpretation; if that is the case, do not hesitate. But do not quibble about insignificant matters. Also, he will usually ask you some question about your education, experience or your present job – partly to get you to start talking and to establish the interviewing "rapport." He may start the actual questioning, or turn it over to one of the other members. Frequently, each member undertakes the questioning on a particular area, one in which he is perhaps most competent, so you can expect each member to participate in the examination. Because time is limited, you may also expect some rather abrupt switches in the direction the questioning takes, so do not be upset by it. Normally, a board member will not pursue a single line of questioning unless he discovers a particular strength or weakness.

After each member has participated, the chairman will usually ask whether any member has any further questions, then will ask you if you have anything you wish to add. Unless you are expecting this question, it may floor you. Worse, it may start you off on an extended, extemporaneous speech. The board is not usually seeking more information. The question is principally to offer you a last opportunity to present further qualifications or to indicate that you have nothing to add. So, if you feel that a significant qualification or characteristic has been overlooked, it is proper to point it out in a sentence or so. Do not compliment the board on the thoroughness of their examination – they have been sketchy, and you know it. If you wish, merely say, "No thank you, I have nothing further to add." This is a point where you can "talk yourself out" of a good impression or fail to present an important bit of information. Remember, *you close the interview yourself.*

The chairman will then say, "That is all, Mr. _____, thank you." Do not be startled; the interview is over, and quicker than you think. Thank him, gather your belongings and take your leave. Save your sigh of relief for the other side of the door.

How to put your best foot forward

Throughout this entire process, you may feel that the board individually and collectively is trying to pierce your defenses, seek out your hidden weaknesses and embarrass and confuse you. Actually, this is not true. They are obliged to make an appraisal of your qualifications for the job you are seeking, and they want to see you in your best light. Remember, they must interview all candidates and a non-cooperative candidate may become a failure in spite of their best efforts to bring out his qualifications. Here are 15 suggestions that will help you:

1) Be natural – Keep your attitude confident, not cocky

If you are not confident that you can do the job, do not expect the board to be. Do not apologize for your weaknesses, try to bring out your strong points. The board is interested in a positive, not negative, presentation. Cockiness will antagonize any board member and make him wonder if you are covering up a weakness by a false show of strength.

2) Get comfortable, but don't lounge or sprawl

Sit erectly but not stiffly. A careless posture may lead the board to conclude that you are careless in other things, or at least that you are not impressed by the importance of the occasion. Either conclusion is natural, even if incorrect. Do not fuss with your clothing, a pencil or an ashtray. Your hands may occasionally be useful to emphasize a point; do not let them become a point of distraction.

3) Do not wisecrack or make small talk

This is a serious situation, and your attitude should show that you consider it as such. Further, the time of the board is limited – they do not want to waste it, and neither should you.

4) Do not exaggerate your experience or abilities

In the first place, from information in the application or other interviews and sources, the board may know more about you than you think. Secondly, you probably will not get away with it. An experienced board is rather adept at spotting such a situation, so do not take the chance.

5) If you know a board member, do not make a point of it, yet do not hide it

Certainly you are not fooling him, and probably not the other members of the board. Do not try to take advantage of your acquaintanceship – it will probably do you little good.

6) Do not dominate the interview

Let the board do that. They will give you the clues – do not assume that you have to do all the talking. Realize that the board has a number of questions to ask you, and do not try to take up all the interview time by showing off your extensive knowledge of the answer to the first one.

7) Be attentive

You only have 20 minutes or so, and you should keep your attention at its sharpest throughout. When a member is addressing a problem or question to you, give him your undivided attention. Address your reply principally to him, but do not exclude the other board members.

8) Do not interrupt

A board member may be stating a problem for you to analyze. He will ask you a question when the time comes. Let him state the problem, and wait for the question.

9) Make sure you understand the question

Do not try to answer until you are sure what the question is. If it is not clear, restate it in your own words or ask the board member to clarify it for you. However, do not haggle about minor elements.

10) Reply promptly but not hastily

A common entry on oral board rating sheets is "candidate responded readily," or "candidate hesitated in replies." Respond as promptly and quickly as you can, but do not jump to a hasty, ill-considered answer.

11) Do not be peremptory in your answers

A brief answer is proper – but do not fire your answer back. That is a losing game from your point of view. The board member can probably ask questions much faster than you can answer them.

12) Do not try to create the answer you think the board member wants

He is interested in what kind of mind you have and how it works – not in playing games. Furthermore, he can usually spot this practice and will actually grade you down on it.

13) Do not switch sides in your reply merely to agree with a board member

Frequently, a member will take a contrary position merely to draw you out and to see if you are willing and able to defend your point of view. Do not start a debate, yet do not surrender a good position. If a position is worth taking, it is worth defending.

14) Do not be afraid to admit an error in judgment if you are shown to be wrong

The board knows that you are forced to reply without any opportunity for careful consideration. Your answer may be demonstrably wrong. If so, admit it and get on with the interview.

15) Do not dwell at length on your present job

The opening question may relate to your present assignment. Answer the question but do not go into an extended discussion. You are being examined for a *new* job, not your present one. As a matter of fact, try to phrase ALL your answers in terms of the job for which you are being examined.

Basis of Rating

Probably you will forget most of these "do's" and "don'ts" when you walk into the oral interview room. Even remembering them all will not ensure you a passing grade. Perhaps you did not have the qualifications in the first place. But remembering them will help you to put your best foot forward, without treading on the toes of the board members.

Rumor and popular opinion to the contrary notwithstanding, an oral board wants you to make the best appearance possible. They know you are under pressure – but they also want to see how you respond to it as a guide to what your reaction would be under the pressures of the job you seek. They will be influenced by the degree of poise you display, the personal traits you show and the manner in which you respond.

ABOUT THIS BOOK

This book contains tests divided into Examination Sections. Go through each test, answering every question in the margin. At the end of each test look at the answer key and check your answers. On the ones you got wrong, look at the right answer choice and learn. Do not fill in the answers first. Do not memorize the questions and answers, but understand the answer and principles involved. On your test, the questions will likely be different from the samples. Questions are changed and new ones added. If you understand these past questions you should have success with any changes that arise. Tests may consist of several types of questions. We have additional books on each subject should more study be advisable or necessary for you. Finally, the more you study, the better prepared you will be. This book is intended to be the last thing you study before you walk into the examination room. Prior study of relevant texts is also recommended. NLC publishes some of these in our Fundamental Series. Knowledge and good sense are important factors in passing your exam. Good luck also helps. So now study this Passbook, absorb the material contained within and take that knowledge into the examination. Then do your best to pass that exam.

———

EXAMINATION SECTION

MECHANICAL APTITUDE
MECHANICAL COMPREHENSION
EXAMINATION SECTION
TEST 1

DIRECTIONS : Each question or incomplete statement below is followed by several suggested answers or completions. Select the *one* that *BEST* answers the question or completes the statement. *PRINT THE LETTER OF THE CORRECT ANSWER IN THE SPACE AT THE RIGHT.*

Questions 1-3.

DIRECTIONS: Questions 1 to 3 inclusive are based upon the following paragraph.

The only openings permitted in fire partitions except openings for ventilating ducts shall be those required for doors. There shall be but one such door opening unless the provision of additional openings would not exceed, in total width of all doorways, 25 percent of the length of the wall. The minimum distance between openings shall be three feet. The maximum area for such a door opening shall be 80 square feet, except that such openings for the passage of motor trucks may be a maximum of 140 square feet.

1.   According to the above paragraph, openings in fire partitions are permitted *only* for   1____

    A.   doors
    B.   doors and windows
    C.   doors and ventilation ducts
    D.   doors, windows and ventilation ducts

2.   In a fire partition, 22 feet long and 10 feet high, the *MAXIMUM* number of doors, 3 feet wide and 7 feet high, is   2____

    A.   1   B.   2   C.   3   D.   4

3.   3____

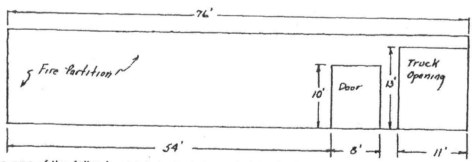

The one of the following statements about the layout shown above that is *MOST* accurate is that the

    A.   total width of the openings is too large
    B.   truck opening is too large
    C.   truck and door openings are too close together
    D.   layout is acceptable

4. At a given temperature, a wet hand will freeze to a bar of metal, but *NOT* to a piece of wood, because the   4_____

    A.   metal expands and contracts more than the wood
    B.   wood is softer than the metal
    C.   wood will burn at a lower temperature than the metal
    D.   metal is a better conductor of heat than the wood

5. Of the following items commonly found in a household, the one that uses the *MOST* electric current is a(n)   5_____

    A.   150-watt light bulb   B.   toaster
    C.   door buzzer   D.   8" electric fan

6. Sand and ashes are frequently placed on icy pavements to prevent skidding. The effect of the sand and ashes is to increase   6_____

    A.   inertia   B.   gravity   C.   momentum   D.   friction

7. The air near the ceiling of a room usually is warmer than the air near the floor because   7_____

    A.   there is better air circulation at the floor level
    B.   warm air is lighter than cold air
    C.   windows usually are nearer the floor than the ceiling
    D.   heating pipes usually run along the ceiling

8.   8_____

DIA. 1   *DIA. 2*

It is safer to use the ladder positioned as shown in diagram 1 than as shown in diagram 2 because, in diagram 1,

    A.   less strain is placed upon the center rungs of the ladder
    B.   it is easier to grip and stand on the ladder
    C.   the ladder reaches a lower height
    D.   the ladder is less likely to tip over backwards

9.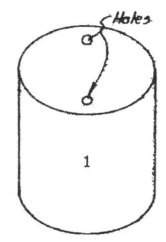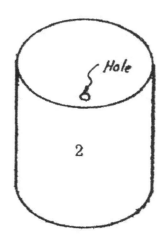

9____

It is *easier* to pour a liquid from:

A. Can 1 because there are two holes from which the liquid can flow
B. Can 1 because air can enter through one hole while the liquid comes out the other hole
C. Can 2 because the liquid comes out under greater pressure
D. Can 2 because it is easier to direct the flow of the liquid when there is only one hole

10. A substance which is subject to "spontaneous combustion" is one that

10____

A. is explosive when heated
B. is capable of catching fire without an external source of heat
C. acts to speed up the burning of material
D. liberates oxygen when heated

11. The sudden shutting down of a nozzle on a hose discharging water under high pressure is a *bad* practice *CHIEFLY* because the

11____

A. hose is likely to whip about violently
B. hose is likely to burst
C. valve handle is likely to snap
D. valve handle is likely to jam

12. Fire can continue where there are present fuel, oxygen from the air or other source, and a sufficiently high temperature to maintain combustion. The method of extinguishment of fire *MOST* commonly used is to

12____

A. remove the fuel
B. exclude the oxygen from the burning material
C. reduce the temperature of the burning material
D. smother the flames of the burning material

13.

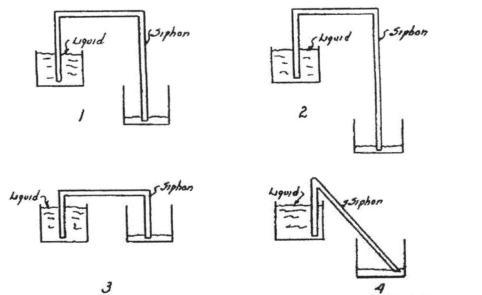

The *one* of the siphon arrangements shown above which would *MOST* quickly transfer a solution from the container on the left side to the one on the right side is numbered

A. 1   B. 2   C. 3   D. 4

14. Static electricity is a hazard in industry CHIEFLY because it may cause

    A. dangerous or painful burns
    B. chemical decomposition of toxic elements
    C. sparks which can start an explosion
    D. overheating of electrical equipment

15.

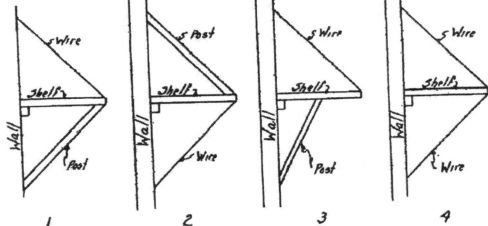

The *STRONGEST* method of supporting the shelf is shown in diagram

A. 1   B. 2   C. 3   D. 4

16. A row boat will float *deeper* in fresh water than in salt water *because*

    A. in the salt water the salt will occupy part of the space
    B. fresh water is heavier than salt water
    C. salt water is heavier than fresh water
    D. salt water offers less resistance than fresh water

16____

17.

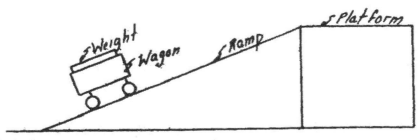

It is easier to get the load onto the platform by using the ramp than it is to lift it directly onto the platform. This is *true* because the effect of the ramp is to

    A. reduce the amount of friction so that less force is required
    B. distribute the weight over a larger area
    C. support part of the load so that less force is needed to move the wagon
    D. increase the effect of the moving weight

17____

18.

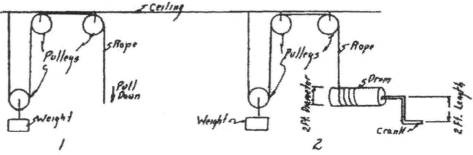

More weight can be lifted by the method shown in diagram 2 than as shown in diagram 1 because

    A. it takes less force to turn a crank than it does to pull in a straight line
    B. the drum will prevent the weight from falling by itself
    C. the length of the crank is larger than the radius of the drum
    D. the drum has more rope on it easing the pull

18____

19.

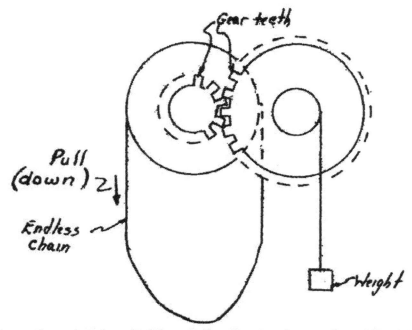

As the endless chain is pulled down in the direction shown, the weight will move

- A. *up* faster than the endless chain is pulled down
- B. *up* slower than the endless chain is pulled down
- C. *down* faster than the endless chain is pulled down
- D. *down* slower than the endless chain is pulled down

20. Two balls of the same size, but different weights, are both dropped from a 10-ft. height. The one of the following statements that is *MOST* accurate is that

- A. both balls will reach the ground at the same time because they are the same size
- B. both balls will reach the ground at the same time because the effect of gravity is the same on both balls
- C. the heavier ball will reach the ground first because it weighs more
- D. the lighter ball will reach the ground first because air resistance is greater on the heavier ball

21. It is considered poor practice to increase the leverage of a wrench by placing a pipe over the handle of the wrench. This is true *PRINCIPALLY* because

- A. the wrench may break
- B. the wrench may slip off the nut
- C. it is harder to place the wrench on the nut
- D. the wrench is more difficult to handle

22.

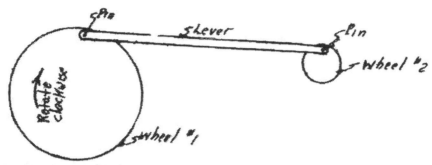

If wheel #1 is turned in the direction shown, wheel #2 will

A. turn continously in a clockwise direction
B. turn continously in a counterclockwise direction
C. move back and fourth
D. became jammed and both wheels will shop

23. ALL SOLID AREAS REPRESENT EQUAL WEIGHTS ATTACHED TO THE FLYWHEEL

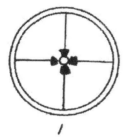 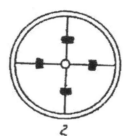 

The above diagrams are of flywheels made of the same material with the same dimensions and attached to similar engines. The solid areas represent equal weights attached to the fly wheel. If all three engines are running at the same speed for the same length of time and the power to the engines is shut of simultaneously,

A. wheel 1 will continue turning longest
B. wheel 2 will continue turning longest
C. wheel 3 will continue turning longest
D. all three wheels will continue turning for the same time

24. The one of the following substance which expands when freezing is

A. alcohol   B. ammonia   C. mercury   D. water

25. A piece of copper wire 30 feet long is cut into two pieces, 20 feet and 10 feet. The resistance of the *longer* piece, compared to the shorter, is

A. one-half as much   B. two-thirds as much
C. one and one-half as much   D. twice as much

KEY (CORRECT ANSWERS)

1.	C		11.	B
2.	A		12.	C
3.	B		13.	B
4.	D		14.	C
5.	B		15.	A
6.	D		16.	C
7.	B		17.	C
8.	D		18.	C
9.	B		19.	D
10.	B		20.	B

21.	A
22.	D
23.	C
24.	D
25.	D

TEST 2

DIRECTIONS: Each question or incomplete statement below is followed by several suggested answers or completions. Select the *one* that *BEST* answers the question or completes the statement. *PRINT THE LETTER OF THE CORRECT ANSWER IN THE SPACE AT THE RIGHT.*

Questions 1-2.

DIRECTIONS: Questions 1 and 2 are to be answered in accordance with the information in the following statement:

The electrical resistance of copper wires varies directly with their lengths and inversely with their cross section areas.

1. A piece of copper wire 30 feet long is cut into two pieces, 20 feet and 10 feet. The resistance of the *longer* piece, compared to the shorter, is   1____

    A. one-half as much
    B. two-thirds as much
    C. one and one-half as much
    D. twice as much

2. Two pieces of copper wire are each 10 feet long but the cross section area of one is 2/3 that of the other. The resistance of the piece with the *larger* cross-section area is   2____

    A. one-half the resistance of the smaller
    B. two-thirds the resistance of the smaller
    C. one and one-half times the resistance of the smaller
    D. twice the resistance of the smaller

3.   3____

The arrangement of the lever which would require the *LEAST* amount of force to move the weight is shown in the diagram numbered

    A. 1   B. 2   C. 3   D. 4

4. Steel supporting beams in buildings often are surrounded by a thin layer of concrete to keep the beams from becoming hot and collapsing during a fire.   4____
   The *one* of the following statements which *BEST* explains how collapse is prevented by this arrangement is that concrete

    A. becomes stronger as its temperature is increased

B. acts as an insulating material
C. protects the beam from rust and corrosion
D. reacts chemically with steel at high temperatures

5. If boiling water is poured into a drinking glass, the glass is likely to crack. If, however, a   5____
metal spoon first is placed in the glass, it is much less likely to crack. The reason that the
glass with the spoon is *less likely* to crack is that the spoon

A. distributes the water over a larger surface of the glass
B. quickly absorbs heat from the water
C. reinforces the glass
D. reduces the amount of water which can be poured into the glass

6. It takes *more* energy to force water through a *long* pipe than through a *short* pipe of the   6____
same diameter. The *PRINCIPAL* reason for this is

A. gravity   B. friction   C. inertia   D. cohesion

7. A pump, discharging at 300 lbs.-per-sq.-inch pressure, delivers water through 100 feet   7____
of pipe laid horizontally. If the valve at the end of the pipe is shut so that no water can
flow, then the pressure at the valve is, for practical purposes,

A. *greater* than the pressure at the pump
B. *equal to* the pressure at the pump
C. *less* than the pressure at the pump
D. *greater or less* than the pressure at the pump, depending on the type of pump used

8. The explosive force of a gas when stored under various pressures is given in the follow-   8____
ing table:

Storage Pressure	Explosive Force
10	1
20	8
30	27
40	64
50	125

The *one* of the following statements which *BEST* expresses the relationship between the
storage pressure and explosive force is that
A. there is no systematic relationship between an increase in storage pressure and
an increase in explosive force
B. the explosive force varies as the square of the pressure
C. the explosive force varies as the cube of the pressure
D. the explosive force varies as the fourth power of the pressure

9.

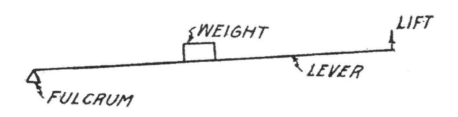

The leverage system in the sketch above is used to raise a weight. In order to *reduce* the amount of force required to raise the weight, it is necessary to

A. decrease the length of the lever
B. place the weight closer to the fulcrum
C. move the weight closer to the person applying the force
D. move the fulcrum further from the weight

10. In the accompanying sketch of a block and fall, if the end of the rope P is pulled so that it moves one foot, the distance the weight will be *raised* is

A. 1/2 ft.
B. 1 ft.
C. 1 1/2 ft.
D. 2 ft.

9_____

10_____

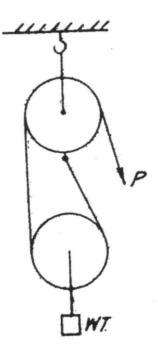

11.   11___

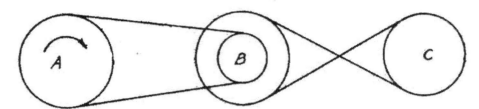

The above sketch diagrammatically shows a pulley and belt system. If pulley A is made to rotate in a clockwise direction, *then* pulley C will rotate

- A.   faster than pulley A and in a clockwise direction
- B.   slower than pulley A and in a clockwise direction
- C.   faster than pulley A and in a counter-clockwise direction
- D.   slower than pulley A and in a counter-clockwise direction

12.   12___

 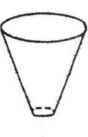 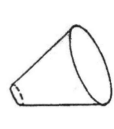 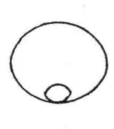

| *1* | *2* | *3* | *4* |

The above diagrams show four positions of the same object. The position in which this object is *MOST* stable is

A.   1   B.   2   C.   3   D.   4

13.   The accompanying sketch dia-   13___
      grammatically shows a system of
      meshing gears with relative diam-
      eters as drawn. If gear 1 is made
      to rotate in the direction of the
      arrow, *then* the gear that will turn
      FASTEST is numbered

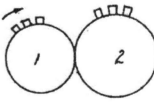 

A.   1   B.   2   C.   3   D.   4

14.

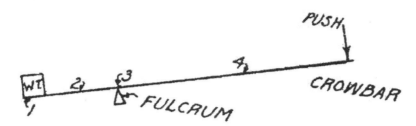

The above sketch shows a weight being lifted by means of a crowbar.
The point at which the tendency for the bar to break is *GREATEST* is

A. 1   B. 2   C. 3   D. 4

15.

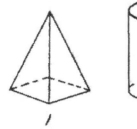 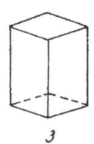 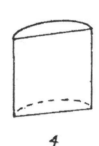

The above sketches show four objects which weigh the same but have different shapes.
The object which is *MOST* difficult to tip over is numbered

A. 1   B. 2   C. 3   D. 4

16.

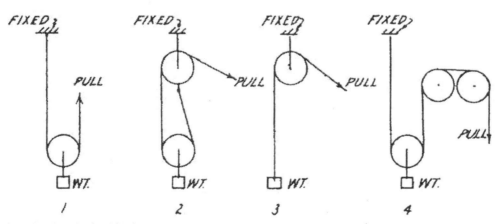

An object is to be lifted by means of a system of lines and pulleys. Of the systems shown above, the *one* which would require the *GREATEST* force to be used in lifting the weight is the one numbered

A. 1   B. 2   C. 3   D. 4

17. An intense fire develops in a room in which carbon dioxide cylinders are stored. The
PRINCIPAL hazard in this situation is that

    17____

    A. the CO_2 may catch fire
    B. toxic fumes may be released
    C. the cylinders may explode
    D. released CO_2 may intensify the fire

18. At a fire involving the roof of a 5-story building, the firemen trained their hose stream on
the fire from a vacant lot across the street, aiming the stream at a point about 15 feet
above the roof.
In this situation, water in the stream would be traveling at the GREATEST speed

    18____

    A. as it leaves the hose nozzle
    B. at a point midway between the ground and the roof
    C. at the maximum height of the stream
    D. as it drops on the roof

19. A principle of lighting is that the intensity of illumination at a point is inversely proportional
to the square of the distance from the source of illumination.
Assume that a pulley lamp is lowered from a position of 6 feet to one of three feet
above a desk. According to the above principle, we would expect that the amount of
illumination reaching the desk from the lamp in the lower position, as compared to the
higher position, will be

    19____

    A. half as much   B. twice as much
    C. four times as much   D. nine times as much

20.

    20____

When standpipes are required in a structure, sufficient risers must be installed so that
no point on the floor is more than 120 feet from a riser.
The one of the above diagrams which gives the MAXIMUM area which can be covered
by one riser is

    A. 1   B. 2   C. 3   D. 4

21. Spontaneous combustion may be the reason for a pile of oily rags catching fire.
In general, spontaneous combustion is the DIRECT result of

    21____

    A. application of flame   B. falling sparks
    C. intense sunlight   D. chemical action
    E. radioactivity

22. In general, firemen are advised not to direct a solid stream of water on fires burning in electrical equipment. Of the following, the *MOST* logical reason for this instruction is that

    A. water is a conductor of electricity
    B. water will do more damage to the electrical equipment than the fire
    C. hydrogen in water may explode when it comes in contact with electric current
    D. water will not effectively extinguish fires in electrical equipment
    E. water may spread the fire to other circuits

22____

23. The height at which a fireboat will float in still water is determined *CHIEFLY* by the

    A. weight of the water displaced by the boat
    B. horsepower of the boat's engines
    C. number of propellers on the boat
    D. curve the bow has above the water line
    E. skill with which the boat is maneuvered

23____

24. When firemen are working at the nozzle of a hose they usually lean forward on the hose. The *most likely* reason for taking this position is that

    A. the surrounding air is cooled, making the firemen more comfortable
    B. a backward force is developed which must be counteracted
    C. the firemen can better see where the stream strikes
    D. the fireman are better protected from injury by falling debris
    E. the stream is projected further

24____

25. In general, the color and odor of smoke will *BEST* indicate

    A. the cause of the fire
    B. the extent of the fire
    C. how long the fire has been burning
    D. the kind of material on fire
    E. the exact seat of the fire

25____

KEY (CORRECT ANSWERS)

1.	D		11.	C
2.	B		12.	A
3.	A		13.	D
4.	B		14.	C
5.	B		15.	A
6.	B		16.	C
7.	B		17.	C
8.	C		18.	A
9.	B		19.	C
10.	A		20.	C

21.	D
22.	A
23.	A
24.	B
25.	D

_____

TEST 3

DIRECTIONS : Each question or incomplete statement below is followed by several suggested answers or completions. Select the *one* that *BEST* answers the question or completes the statement. *PRINT THE LETTER OF THE CORRECT ANSWER IN THE SPACE AT THE RIGHT.*

1. As a demonstration, firemen set up two hose lines identical in every respect except that one was longer than the other. Water was then delivered through these lines from one pump and it was seen that the stream from the longer hose line had a shorter "throw," Of the following, the *MOST* valid explanation of this difference in "throw" is that the

    1____

   A. air resistance to the water stream is proportional to the length of hose
   B. time required for water to travel through the longer hose is greater than for the shorter one
   C. loss due to friction is greater in the longer hose than in the shorter one
   D. rise of temperature is greater in the longer hose than in the shorter one
   E. longer hose line probably developed a leak at one of the coupling joints

2. Of the following toxic gases, the *one* which is *MOST* dangerous because it cannot be seen and has no odor, is

    2____

   A. ether
   D. ammonia
   B. carbon monoxide
   E. cooking gas
   C. chlorine

3. You are visiting with some friends when their young son rushes into the room with his clothes on fire. You immediately wrap him in a rug and roll him on the floor. The *MOST* important reason for your action is that the

    3____

   A. flames are confined within the rug
   B. air supply to the fire is reduced
   C. burns sustained will be third degree, rather than first degree
   D. whirling action will put out the fire
   E. boy will not suffer from shock

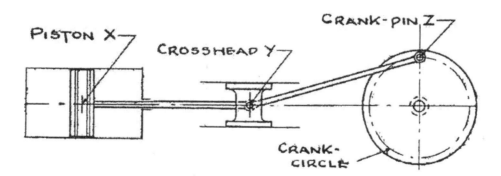

FIGURE I

Questions 4-6,

DIRECTIONS: The device shown in Figure I above represents schematically a mechanism
               commonly used to change reciprocating (back and forth) motion to rotation
               (circular) motion.
    The following questions, numbered 4 to 6 inclusive, are to be answered with reference to
    this device.

4. Assume that piston X is placed in its extreme left position so that X, Y and Z are in a hor-   4____
    izontal line. If a horizontal force to the right is applied to the piston X, we may then expect
    that

    A.   the crank-pin Z will revolve clockwise
    B.   the crosshead Y will move in a direction opposite to that of X
    C.   the crank-pin Z will revolve counterclockwise
    D.   no movement will take place
    E.   the crank-pin Z will oscillate back and forth

5. If we start from the position shown in the above diagram, and move piston X to the right,   5____
    the result will be that

    A.   the crank-pin Z will revolve counterclockwise and cross-head Y will move to the left
    B.   the crank-pin Z will revolve clockwise and crosshead Y will move to the left
    C.   the crank-pin Z will revolve clockwise and crosshead Y will move to the right
    D.   the crank-pin Z will revolve clockwise and crosshead Y will move to the right
    E.   crosshead Y will move to the left as piston X moves to the right

6. If crank-pin Z is moved closer to the center of the crank circle, then the length of the   6____

    A.   stroke of piston X is increased
    B.   stroke of piston X is decreased
    C.   stroke of piston X is unchanged
    D.   rod between the piston X and crosshead Y is increased
    E.   rod between the piston X and crosshead Y is decreased

Questions 7-8.

DIRECTIONS: Figure II represents schematically a block-and-fall tackle. The advantage
               derived from this machine is that the effect of the applied force is multiplied by
               the number of lines of rope directly supporting the load. The following two
               questions, numbered 7 and 8, are to be answered with reference to this figure.

7. Pull P is exerted on line T to raise the load L. The line in which the *LARGEST* strain is   7____
    finally induced is line

    A. T   B. U   C. V   D. X   E. Y

8. If the largest pull P that two men can apply to line T is 280 lbs., the *MAXI-MUM* load L that they can raise without regard to frictional losses is, *most nearly,* _____ lbs.

    A. 1960
    B. 1680
    C. 1400
    D. 1260
    E. 1120

8 _____

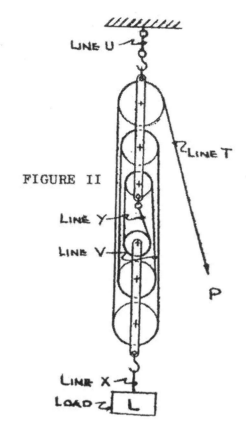

FIGURE II

Questions 9-13.

DIRECTIONS: Answer Questions 9 to 13 on the basis of Figure III. The diagram schematically illustrates part of a water tank. 1 and 5 are outlet and inlet pipes, respectively. 2 is a valve which can be used to open and close the outlet pipe by hand. 3 is a float which is rigidly connected to valve 4 by an iron bar, thus causing that valve to open or shut as the float rises or falls 4 is a hinged valve which controls the flow of water into the tank.

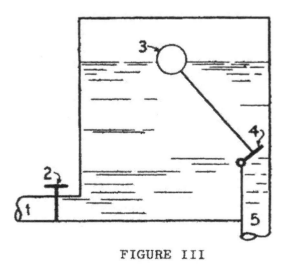

FIGURE III

9. If the tank is half filled and water is going out of pipe 1 more rapidly than it is coming in   9.___
    through pipe 5, *then*

    A. valve 2 is closed   B. float 3 is rising in the tank
    C. valve 4 is opening wider   D. valve 4 is closed
    E. float 3 is stationary

10. If the tank is half filled with water and water is coming in through inlet pipe 5 more rapidly   10.___
    than it is going out through outlet pipe 1, *then*

    A. valve 2 is closed   B. float 3 is rising in the tank
    C. valve 4 is opening wider   D. valve 4 is closed
    E. float 3 is stationary

11. If the tank is empty, then it can *normally* be expected that   11.___

    A. float 3 is at its highest position
    B. float 3 is at its lowest position
    C. valve 2 is closed
    D. valve 4 is closed
    E. water will not come into the tank

12. If float 3 develops a leak, *then*   12.___

    A. the tank will tend to empty
    B. water will tend to stop coming into the tank
    C. valve 4 will tend to close
    D. valve 2 will tend to close
    E. valve 4 will tend to remain open

13. Without any other changes being made, if the bar joining the float to valve 4 is removed   13.___
    and a slightly shorter bar substituted, *then*

    A. a smaller quantity of water in the tank will be required before the float closes valve
        4
    B. valve 4 will not open
    C. valve 4 will not close
    D. it is not possible to determine what will happen
    E. a greater quantity of water in the tank will be required before the float closes
        valve 4

Questions 14-18.

DIRECTIONS: Answer Questions 14 to 18 on the basis of Figure IV. A, B, C and D are four
              meshed gears forming a gear train. Gear A is the driver. Gears A and D each
              have twice as many teeth as gear B, and gear C has four times as many teeth
              as gear B. The diagram is schematic: the teeth go all around each gear.

14. *Two* gears which turn in the *same* direction are: 14.___

    A. A and B   B. B and C   C. C and D
    D. D and A   E. B and D

15. The *two* gears which
    revolve at the *same* speed
    are gears

15_____

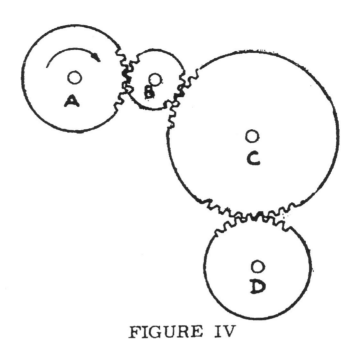

FIGURE IV

    A. A and C   B. A and D   C. B and C
    D. B and D   E. D and C

16. If all the teeth on gear C are stripped without affecting the teeth on gears A, B, and D,   16_____
    then rotation would occur *only* in gear(s)

    A. C   B. D   C. A and B
    D. A, B, and D   E. B and D

17. If gear D is rotating at the rate of 100 RPM, then gear B is rotating at the rate of _____   17_____
    RPM.

    A. 25   B. 50   C. 100   D. 200   E. 400

18. If gear A turns at the rate of two revolutions per second, then the number of revolutions   18_____
    per second that gear C turns is

    A. 1   B. 2   C. 3   D. 4   E. 8

Questions 19-23.

DIRECTIONS: Answer Questions 19 to 23 on the basis of Figure V. The diagram shows a water pump in cross section: 1 is a check valve, 2 and 3 are the spring and diaphragm, respectively, of the discharge valve, 4 is the pump piston; 5 is the inlet valve, and 6 is the pump cylinder. All valves permit the flow of water in one direction only.

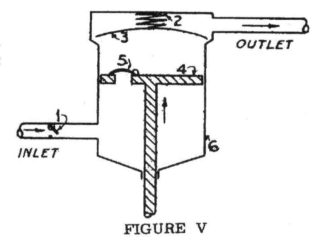

FIGURE V

19. When water is flowing through the outlet pipe,

    A. check valve 1 is closed   B. diaphragm 3 is closed
    C. valve 5 is closed   D. spring 2 is fully extended
    E. the piston is on the downstroke

19____

20. If valve 5 does not work properly and stays closed, *then*

    A. the piston cannot move down   B. the piston cannot move up
    C. diaphragm 3 cannot open   D. check valve 1 cannot close
    E. the flow of water will be reversed

20____

21. If diaphragm 3 does not work properly and stays in the open position, *then*

    A. check valve 1 will not open
    B. valve 5 will not open
    C. spring 2 will be compressed
    D. spring 2 will be extended
    E. water will not flow through the inlet pipe

21____

22. When valve 5 is open during normal operation of the pump, *then*

    A. spring 2 is fully compressed
    B. the piston is on the upstroke
    C. water is flowing through check valve 1
    D. a vacuum is formed between the piston and the bottom of the cylinder
    E. diaphragm 3 is closed

22____

23. If check valve 1 jams and stays closed, *then*

    A. valve 5 will be open on both the upstroke and down stroke of the piston
    B. a vacuum will tend to form in the inlet pipe between the source of the water supply and check valve 1
    C. pressure on the cylinder side of check valve 1 will increase

23____

D. less force will be required to move the piston down
E. more force will be required to move the piston down

24. The one of the following which *BEST* explains why smoke usually rises from a fire is that   24____

A. cooler, heavier air displaces lighter, warm air
B. heat energy of the fire propels the smoke upward
C. suction from the upper air pulls the smoke upward
D. burning matter is chemically changed into heat energy

25. The practice of racing a car engine to warm it up in cold weather, generally, is   25____

A. *good, MAINLY* because repeated stalling of the engine and drain on the battery is avoided
B. *bad, MAINLY* because too much gas is used to get the engine heated
C. *good, MAINLY* because the engine becomes operational in the shortest period of time
D. *bad, MAINLY* because proper lubrication is not established rapidly enough

---

KEY (CORRECT ANSWERS)

1. C		11. B	
2. B		12. E	
3. B		13. A	
4. D		14. E	
5. D		15. B	
6. B		16. C	
7. B		17. D	
8. B		18. A	
9. C		19. C	
10. B		20. A	

21. C
22. E
23. D
24. A
25. D

MECHANICAL APTITUDE

EXAMINATION SECTION
TEST 1

MECHANICAL COMPREHENSION

DIRECTIONS: Questions 1 to 4 test your ability to understand general mechanical devices. Pictures are shown and questions asked about the mechanical devices shown in the picture. Read each question and study the picture. Each question is followed by four choices. For each question, choose the one BEST answer (A, B, C, or D). Then *PRINT THE LETTER OF THE CORRECT ANSWER IN THE SPACE AT THE RIGHT.*

1. The reason for crossing the belt connecting these wheels is to   1.____

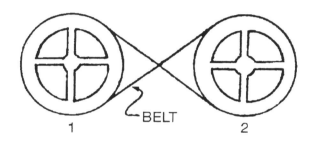

   A.   make the wheels turn in opposite directions
   B.   make wheel 2 turn faster than wheel 1
   C.   save wear on the belt
   D.   take up slack in the belt

2. The purpose of the small gear between the two large gears is to   2.____

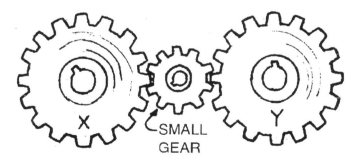

   A.   increase the speed of the larger gears
   B.   allow the larger gears to turn in different directions
   C.   decrease the speed of the larger gears
   D.   make the larger gears turn in the same direction

3. Each of these three-foot-high water cans have a bottom with an area of-one square foot.
   The pressure on the bottom of the cans is

3.____

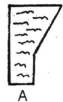  

A   B   C

A.   least in A   B.   least in B
C.   least in C   D.   the same in all

4. The reading on the scale should be   4.____

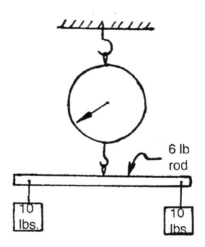

6 lb
rod

10 lbs.   10 lbs

A.   zero
B.   10 pounds
C.   13 pounds
D.   26 pounds

_____

KEY (CORRECT ANSWERS)

1.   A
2.   D
3.   D
4.   D

_____

TEST 2

DIRECTIONS: Questions 1 to 6 test knowledge of tools and how to use them. For each question, decide which one of the four things shown in the boxes labeled A, B, C, or D normally is used with or goes best with the thing in the picture on the left. Then *PRINT THE LETTER OF THE CORRECT ANSWER IN THE SPACE AT THE RIGHT.*

NOTE: All tools are NOT drawn to the same scale.

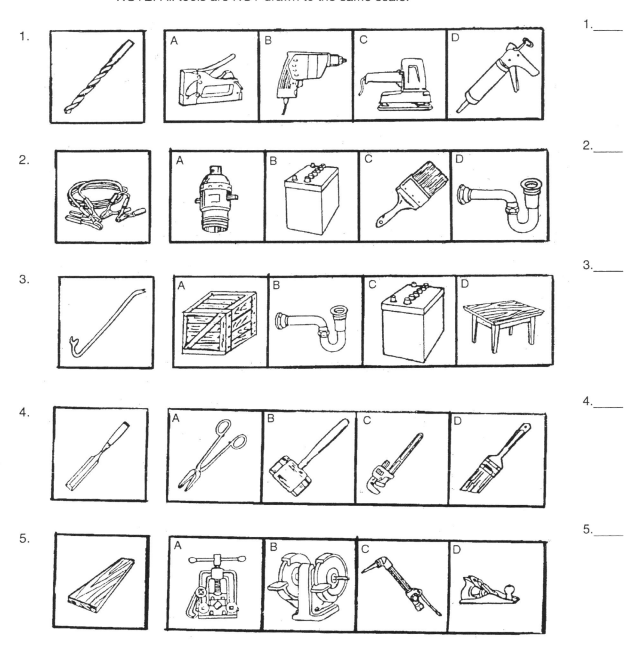

1.____

2.____

3.____

4.____

5.____

6.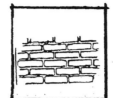

6.____

KEY (CORRECT ANSWERS)

1. B
2. B
3. A

4. B
5. D
6. B

MECHANICAL APTITUDE

EXAMINATION SECTION
TEST 1

QUESTIONS 1-6.

Questions 1 through 6 are questions designed to test your ability to distinguish identical forms from unlike forms.

In each question, there are five drawings, lettered A, B, C, D, and E. Four of the drawings are alike. You are to find the one drawing that is different from the other four in the question. Then, on the Answer Sheet, blacken the space lettered the same as the figure that you have selected.

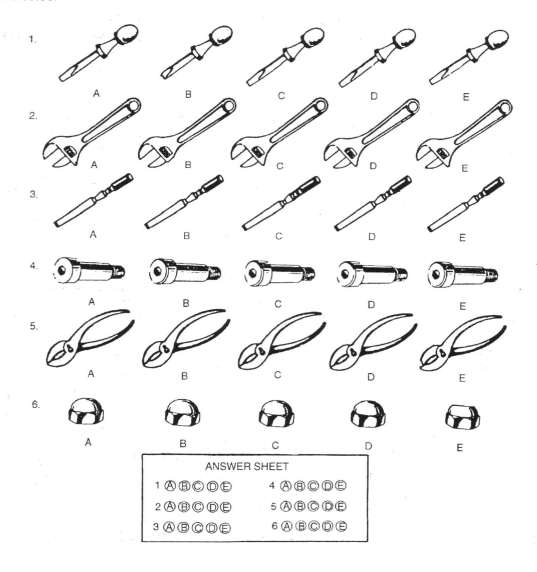

```
ANSWER SHEET
1 Ⓐ Ⓑ Ⓒ Ⓓ Ⓔ      4 Ⓐ Ⓑ Ⓒ Ⓓ Ⓔ
2 Ⓐ Ⓑ Ⓒ Ⓓ Ⓔ      5 Ⓐ Ⓑ Ⓒ Ⓓ Ⓔ
3 Ⓐ Ⓑ Ⓒ Ⓓ Ⓔ      6 Ⓐ Ⓑ Ⓒ Ⓓ Ⓔ
```

QUESTIONS 7-8.

Questions 7 and 8 are questions designed to test your knowledge of pattern matching.

Questions 7 and 8 present problems found in making patterns. Each shows, at the left side, two or more separate flat pieces. In each question, select the arrangement lettered A, B, C, or D that shows how these pieces at the left can be fitted together without gaps or overlapping. The pieces may be turned around or turned over in any way to make them fit together.

On the Answer Sheet blacken the space lettered the same as the figure that you have selected.

Now, look at the questions below.

7. From these pieces, which one of these arrangements can you make?

A   B   C   D

In question 7, only the arrangement D can be made from the pieces shown at the left, so space D is marked for Question 7 on the answer sheet below. (Note that it is necessary to turn the pieces around so that the short sides are at the bottom in the arrangement lettered D. None of the other arrangements show pieces of the given size and shape.)

8. From these pieces, which one of these arrangements can you make?

A   B   C   D

```
ANSWER SHEET

7 Ⓐ Ⓑ Ⓒ Ⓓ
8 Ⓐ Ⓑ Ⓒ Ⓓ
```

30

QUESTIONS 9-10.

Questions 9 and 10. are questions designed to test your ability to identify forms of *LIKE* and *UNLIKE* proportions.

In each of the questions, select from the drawings of objects labeled A, B, C, and D, the one that would have the Top, Front, and Right views shown in the drawing at the left. Then on your Answer Sheet blacken the space that has the same letter as your answer.

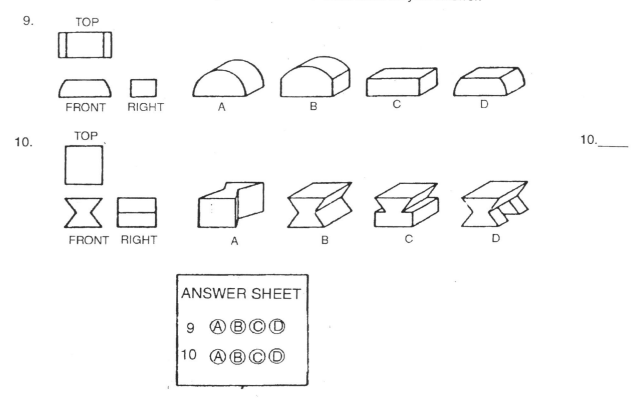

9. TOP / FRONT RIGHT / A B C D

10. TOP / FRONT RIGHT / A B C D

10.____

ANSWER SHEET

9 Ⓐ Ⓑ Ⓒ Ⓓ

10 Ⓐ Ⓑ Ⓒ Ⓓ

QUESTIONS 11-14.

Explanation and Commentary:

In each question, *ONE* rectangle is clearly *WRONG*. For each question, use the measuirng gage to check each of the rectangles and to find the *WRONG* one. Do this by putting the measuring gage rectangle on the question rectangle with the same letter so that the rectangles slightly overlap and the thin lines are parallel, like the one at the right. In this case, the height of the question rectangle exactly matches the height of the measuring gage rectangle, so the question rectangle is the right height. In this case, you do *NOT* mark your answer sheet.

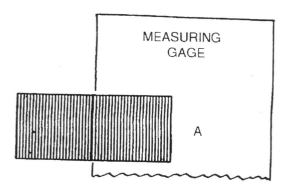

MEASURING GAGE

A

Once in every question, when you put a measuring gage rectangle on a question rectangle, you will find that the heights do *NOT* match and that the question rectangle is clearly wrong, like the one at the right. In this case, you mark on the answer sheet the space with the same letter as the wrong rectangle. *REMEMBER TO LINE UP THE MEASURING RECTANGLE WITH EACH QUESTION RECTANGLE SO THAT THE THIN LINES ARE EXACTLY PARALLEL.*

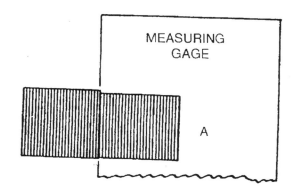

Now, cut out the measuring gage on the last page and practice on the questions. The test will be timed, so practice doing them rapidly and accurately.

Questions 11 through 14 test how quickly and accurately you can check the heights of rectangles with a measuring gage. Each question has five rectangles of different heights. The height is the dimension that runs the same way as the thin lines.

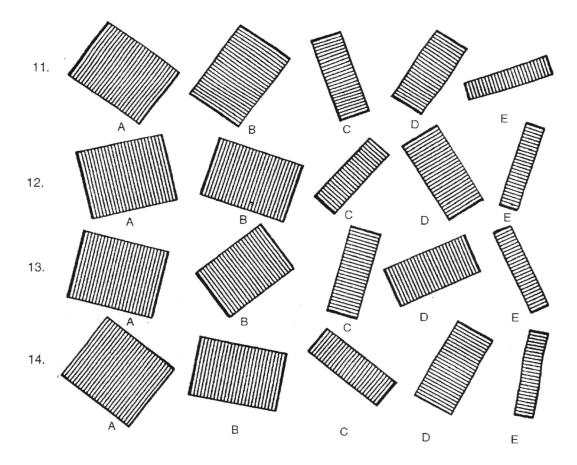

ANSWER SHEET

11 Ⓐ Ⓑ Ⓒ Ⓓ Ⓔ

12 Ⓐ Ⓑ Ⓒ Ⓓ Ⓔ

13 Ⓐ Ⓑ Ⓒ Ⓓ Ⓔ

14 Ⓐ Ⓑ Ⓒ Ⓓ Ⓔ

MEASURING
GAGE

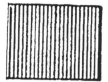 A

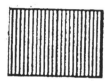 B

 C

 D

 E

KEY (CORRECT ANSWERS)

1.	B	8.	B
2.	B	9.	D
3.	C	10.	B
4.	A	11.	D
5.	E	12.	C
6.	E	13.	B
7.	D	14.	A

EXAMINATION SECTION
TEST 1

DIRECTIONS: Each question or incomplete statement is followed by two suggested answers or completions. Select A or B, or C if the two figures have the same value, as the BEST answer that completes the statement or completes the statement. *PRINT THE LETTER OF THE CORRECT ANSWER IN THE SPACE AT THE RIGHT.*

1.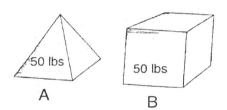
   With which windlass can a man raise the heavier weight?

   1.____

2.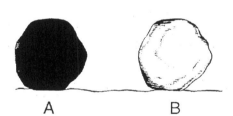
   Which of these solid blocks will be the harder to tip over?

   2.____

3.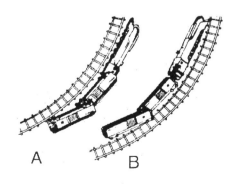
   Which rock will get hotter in the sun?

   3.____

4.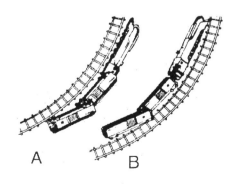

   4.____

   Which of these is the more likely picture of a train wreck?

5.

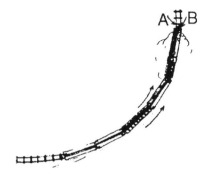

If the track is exactly level, on which rail does more pressure come?

5.____

6.

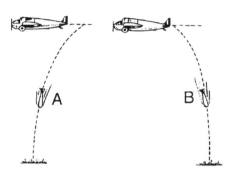

Which picture shows the way a bomb falls from a moving airplane if there is no wind?

6.____

7.

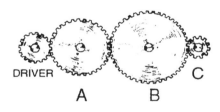

Indicate a gear which turn the same direction as the driver.

7.____

8.

If there are no clouds, on which night will you be able to see more stars?

8.____

9.

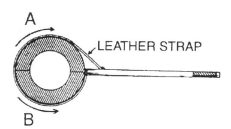

This wrench can be used to turn the pipe in direction:

9.____

10.

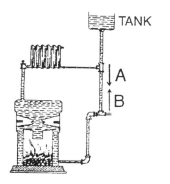

In which direction does the water in the right-hand pipe go?

10.____

11.

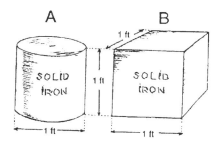

Which weighs more?

11.____

12.

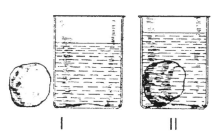

If the rock and tank of water together in picture I weigh 100 pounds, what will they weigh in picture II?

12.____

13.

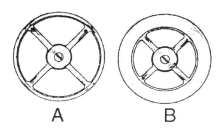

Which steel wheel will keep going longer after the power has been shut off?

13.____

14.

The top of the wheel *X* will go
 A. steadily to the right
 B. steadily to the left
 C. by jerks to the left

14._____

15.

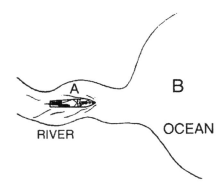

At which point will the boat be lower in the water?

15._____

16.

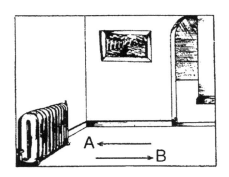

Which arrow shows the way the air will move along the floor when the radiator is turned on?

16._____

17.

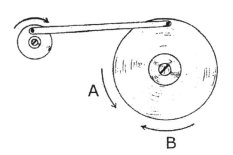

When the little wheel turns around, the big wheel will
 A. turn in direction A
 B. turn in direction B
 C. move back and forth

17._____

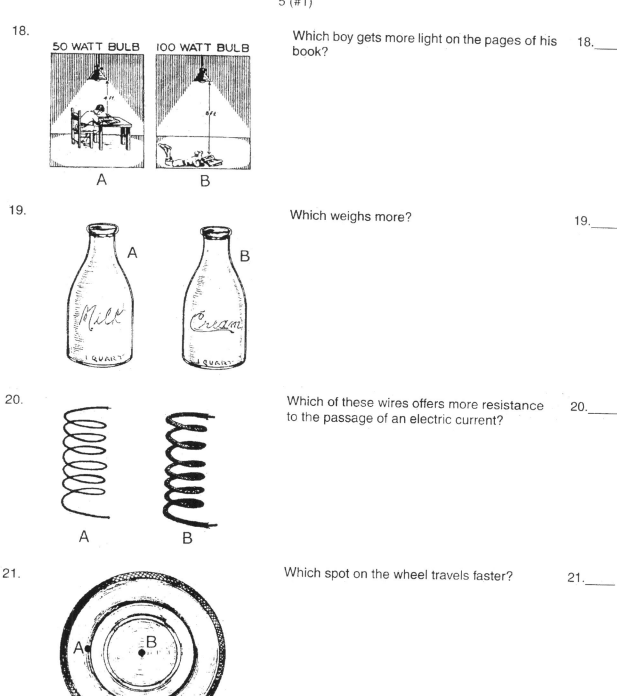

18. Which boy gets more light on the pages of his book?   18.____

19. Which weighs more?   19.____

20. Which of these wires offers more resistance to the passage of an electric current?   20.____

21. Which spot on the wheel travels faster?   21.____

22.

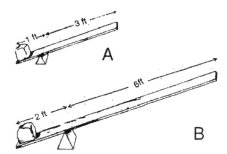

With which arrangement can a man lift the heavier weight?

22.____

23.

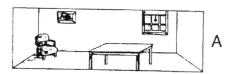

Which room has more of an echo?

23.____

24.

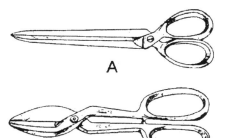

Which would be the BETTER shears for cutting metal?

24.____

KEY (CORRECT ANSWERS)

1.	A		11.	B
2.	A		12.	C
3.	A		13.	B
4.	A		14.	C
5.	B		15.	A
6.	A		16.	A
7.	B		17.	C
8.	B		18.	A
9.	A		19.	A
10.	A		20.	A

21.	B
22.	B
23.	A
24.	B

MECHANICAL APTITUDE
TOOL RECOGNITION AND USE

EXAMINATION SECTION
TEST 1

DIRECTIONS: Each question or incomplete statement below is followed by several suggested answers or completions. Select the one that *BEST* answers the question or completes the statement.

KEY : CORRECT ANSWERS APPEAR AT THE END OF THIS TEST.

1.

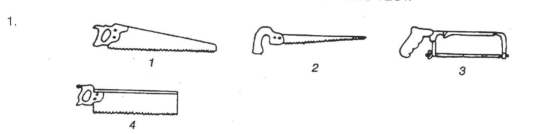

1.____

The saw that is used principally where curved cuts are to be made is numbered

1. 1   2. 2   3. 3   4. 4

2.

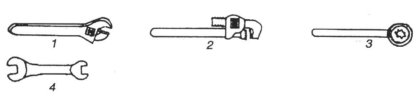

2.____

The wrench that is used principally for pipe work is numbered

1. 1   2. 2   3. 3   4. 4

3.

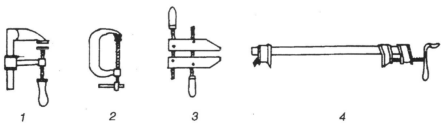

3.____

The carpenter's "hand screw" is numbered

1. 1   2. 2   3. 3   4. 4

4.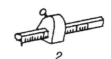

The tool used to measure the depth of a hole is numbered

   1. 1   2. 2   3. 3   4. 4

4._____

5.

The tool that is best suited for use with a wood chisel is numbered

   1. 1   2. 2   3. 3   4. 4

5._____

6.

The screw head that would be tightened with an "Allen" wrench is numbered

   1. 1   2. 2   3. 3   4. 4

6._____

7.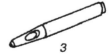

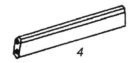

The center punch is numbered

   1. 1   2. 2   3. 3   4. 4

7._____

8.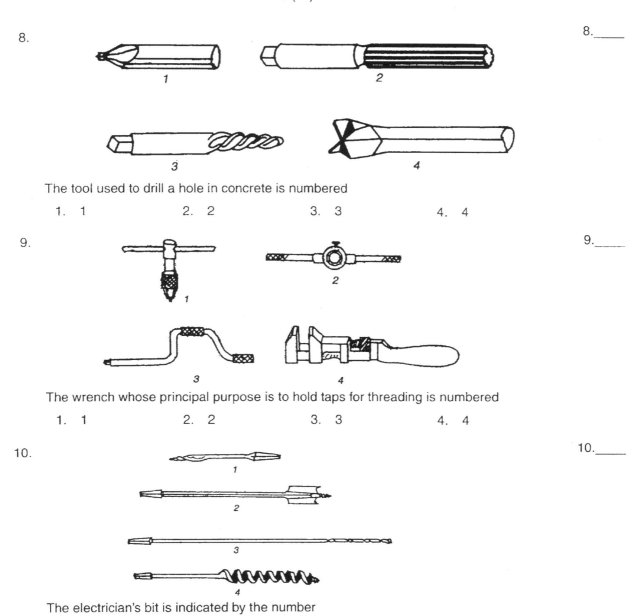

8.____

The tool used to drill a hole in concrete is numbered

1. 1   2. 2   3. 3   4. 4

9.

9.____

The wrench whose principal purpose is to hold taps for threading is numbered

1. 1   2. 2   3. 3   4. 4

10.

10.____

The electrician's bit is indicated by the number

1. 1   2. 2   3. 3   4. 4

11. The head of a cold chisel is "mushroomed" as shown in the sketch.   11.____
    The use of a chisel in this condition is poor practice because
    1. it is impossible to hit the head squarely
    2. the chisel will not cut accurately
    3. chips might fly from the head
    4. the chisel has lost its "temper"

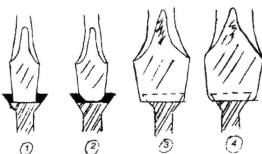

12. The above diagrams show a section of a screw with a screwdriver that is to be used with   12.____
    the screw. The one of the diagrams that shows the correct shape of screwdriver is

    1. 1   2. 2   3. 3   4. 4

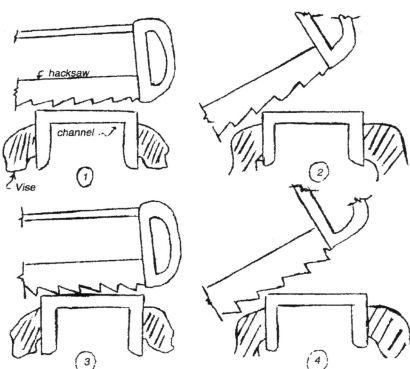

13. A steel channel is to be cut through with a hacksaw. The correct method for doing this is 13.____
shown in the diagram numbered (diagrams above)

   1. 1   2. 2   3. 3   4. 4

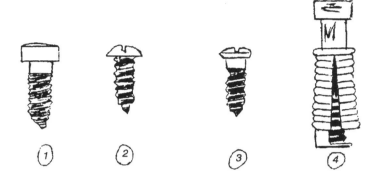

14. The screw above that is most frequently used for sheet metal work is numbered 14.____

   1. 1   2. 2   3. 3   4. 4

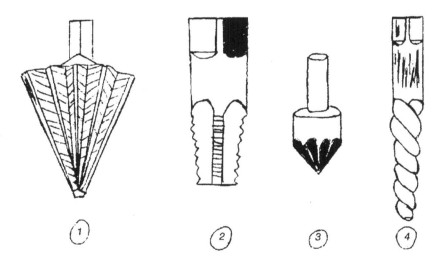

15. The tool used to ream the ends of pipe after the pipe has been cut is shown above in the diagram numbered   15.____

    1. 1   2. 2   3. 3   4. 4

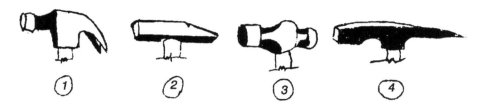

16. The hammer that would be used by a mason to trim brick is shown in the above diagram numbered   16.____

    1. 1   2. 2   3. 3   4. 4

17. The saw intended especially to make accurate miter cuts is shown in the above diagram numbered   17.____

    1. 1   2. 2   3. 3   4. 4

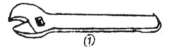 

18. A wrench used to tighten cylinder head bolts to a specified torque is shown in the above diagram numbered

18.____

   1. 1   2. 2   3. 3   4. 4

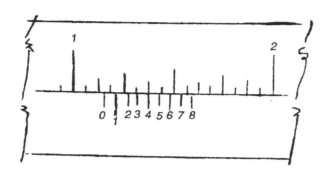

19. A section of the scale of a vernier caliper is shown above. The reading of this caliper setting is most nearly

19.____

   1. 1 3/8   2. 1 5/64   3. 1 5/32   4. 1 7/64

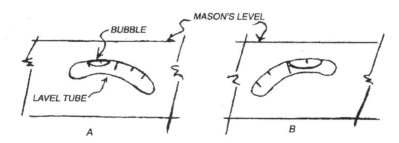

20. A level is placed on a table and the bubble moves to the position indicated in diagram A above. The level is then turned end for end and placed in the same location on the table as before. The bubble now appears as shown in diagram B. The one of the following statements that is correct is

20.____

   1. the left end of the table is higher than the right end
   2. the right end of the table is higher than the left end
   3. it is impossible to tell which end of the table is higher
   4. the level tube is not set properly in the level

21. The flat-head screw is No.

21.____

   1. 1   2. 2   3. 3   4. 4

22. The "Phillips" head is No.   22.____

    1. 1   2. 2   3. 3   4. 4

23. The standard coupling for rigid electrical conduit is   23.____

    1. 1   2. 2   3. 3   4. 4

24. The shape of nut most commonly used on electrical terminals is 24.____

    1. 1   2. 2   3. 3   4. 4

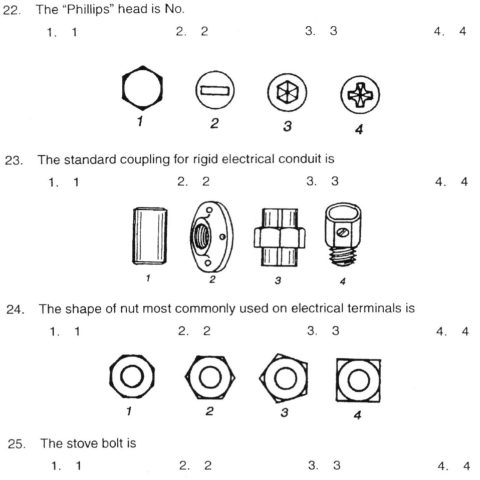

25. The stove bolt is   25.____

    1. 1   2. 2   3. 3   4. 4

KEY (CORRECT ANSWERS)

1.	2		11.	3
2.	2		12.	1
3.	3		13.	1
4.	3		14.	2
5.	4		15.	1
6.	3		16.	4
7.	1		17.	3
8.	4		18.	4
9.	1		19.	3
10.	3		20.	4

21.	3
22.	4
23.	1
24.	2
25.	3

TOOLS

EXAMINATION SECTION
TEST 1

DIRECTIONS: Each question or incomplete statement is followed by several suggested answers or completions. Select the one that BEST answers the question or completes the statement. *PRINT THE LETTER OF THE CORRECT ANSWER IN THE SPACE AT THE RIGHT.*

1. It is NOT good practice to cut thin-walled copper tubing with an ordinary three-wheel pipe cutter because

    A. the cutters will be dulled
    B. too much time is required
    C. the tubing end must be reamed after cutting
    D. the tubing is likely to collapse

1.____

2. Wedges are used under vertical shoring timbers to

    A. utilize scrap wood
    B. permit the use of very short timbers
    C. obtain rigid shoring
    D. absorb construction noise

2.____

3. The LONGEST nail of the following is a _____-penny nail.

    A. 12   B. 10   C. 6   D. 4

3.____

4. A commonly used priming coat for structural steel is

    A. enamel   B. varnish   C. red lead   D. lacquer

4.____

5. A nail set is a tool used for

    A. straightening bent nails
    B. cutting nails to specified size
    C. sinking a nail head in wood
    D. measuring nail size

5.____

6. The sketch at the right shows a gauge used to
    A. measure the depth of a hole
    B. determine if a board has been smoothly planed
    C. check the width of a brick
    D. scribe a line on a board parallel to its edge

GAUGE

6.____

7. The gauge box shown at the right is used for measuring the dry volume of a concrete mix. If the gauge box is to have a volume of 1 cubic yard, dimension H must be APPROXIMATELY _____ feet.

    A. 2.39
    B. 1.69
    C. 1.45
    D. .63

7._____

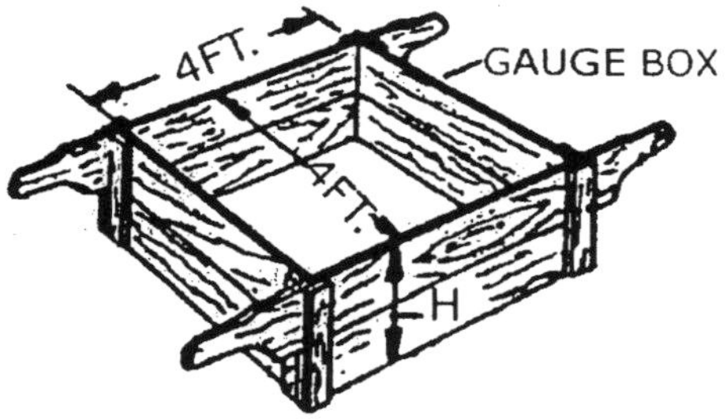

Questions 8-27.

DIRECTIONS: Questions 8 through 27 refer to the use of tools shown below. Refer to these tools when answering these questions.

3 (#1)

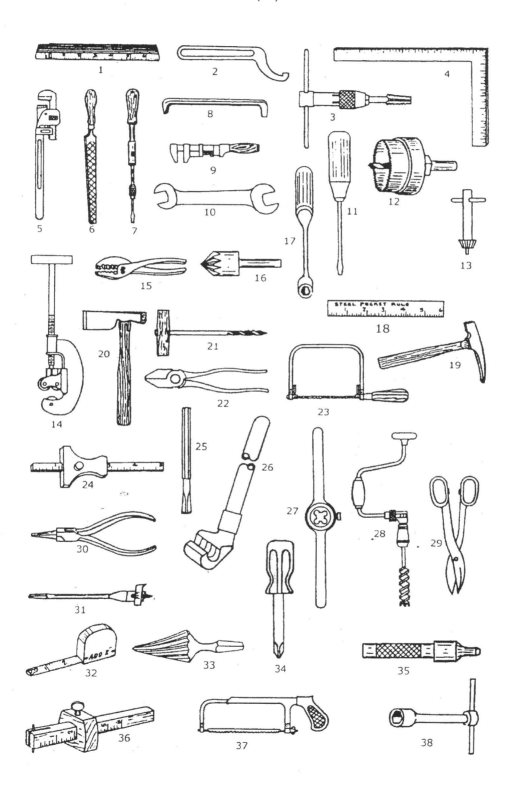

1
2
3
4
5
6
7
8
9
10
11
12
13
14
15
16
17
18
19
20
21
22
23
24
25
26
27
28
29
30
31
32
33
34
35
36
37
38

STEEL POCKET RULE

4 (#1)

8. Tool number 38 is properly called a(n) _____ wrench.   8._____
   A. box   B. open-end   C. socket   D. tool

9. Two tools which are used for cutting large circular holes in thin sheets are numbers   9._____
_____ and _____.
   A. 12; 31   B. 28; 33   C. 12; 28   D. 31; 33

10. If there is a possible danger of electric shock when you are taking measurements, it   10._____
would be BEST to use number
   A. 1   B. 4   C. 18   D. 32

11. A 1/2-inch steel pipe is preferably cut with number   11._____
   A. 14   B. 23   C. 27   D. 29

12. A nut for a #8 machine screw should be tightened using number   12._____
   A. 9   B. 15   C. 17   D. 38

13. The hexagon nut for a 1/2-inch diameter machine bolt should be tightened using number   13._____
   A. 5   B. 10   C. 22   D. 26

14. If a small piece must be chipped off a brick in order to clear an obstruction when a brick   14._____
wall is being built, the MOST suitable tool to use is number
   A. 16   B. 19   C. 20   D. 33

15. A large number of wood screws can be screwed into a board MOST quickly by using   15._____
number
   A. 7   B. 8   C. 11   D. 17

16. A number of different diameter holes can be MOST easily bored through a heavy wood   16._____
plank by using number
   A. 3   B. 13   C. 21   D. 31

17. The tool to use in order to form threads in a hole in a steel block is number   17._____
   A. 2   B. 3   C. 27   D. 31

18. Curved designs in thin wood are preferably cut with number   18._____
   A. 12   B. 23   C. 29   D. 37

19. The driving of Phillips-head screws requires the use of number   19._____
   A. 7   B. 8   C. 11   D. 34

20. In order to properly flare one end of a piece of copper tubing, the tool to use is number   20._____
   A. 13   B. 25   C. 33   D. 35

21. Tool number 16 is used for   21._____
   A. counterboring   B. cutting concrete
   C. countersinking   D. reaming

56

22. A tool that can be used to drill a hole in a concrete wall to install a lead anchor is number 22.____

    A. 3   B. 16   C. 21   D. 25

23. After cutting a piece of steel pipe, the burrs are BEST removed from the inside edge with 23.____
number

    A. 6   B. 13   C. 16   D. 33

24. The MOST convenient tool for measuring the depth of a 1/2-inch diameter hole is num- 24.____
ber

    A. 24   B. 31   C. 32   D. 36

25. A 1" x 1" x 1/8" angle iron would usually be cut using number 25.____

    A. 12   B. 26   C. 29   D. 37

26. Wood screws located in positions NOT accessible to an ordinary screwdriver would be 26.____
removed using number

    A. 2   B. 8   C. 13   D. 30

27. A small hole can be quickly bored through an 1/8-inch thick plywood board with number 27.____

    A. 3   B. 7   C. 21   D. 31

28. The hammer shown to the right would be used by a 28.____
    A. carpenter
    B. bricklayer
    C. tinsmith
    D. plumber

29. Which of the following pairs of tools would be used to tighten a nut on a screw? 29.____

    A. Two open-end wrenches
    B. One open-end wrench and one adjustable wrench
    C. A screwdriver and a wrench
    D. A vise wrench and an adjustable screwdriver

30. In order to determine if a surface is truly horizontal, it should be checked with a 30.____

    A. carpenter's square   B. plumb bob
    C. steel rule   D. spirit level

KEY (CORRECT ANSWERS)

1.	D		16.	D
2.	C		17.	B
3.	A		18.	B
4.	C		19.	D
5.	C		20.	D
6.	D		21.	C
7.	B		22.	D
8.	C		23.	D
9.	A		24.	A
10.	A		25.	D
11.	A		26.	B
12.	C		27.	C
13.	B		28.	B
14.	B		29.	C
15.	A		30.	D

TEST 2

DIRECTIONS: Each question or incomplete statement is followed by several suggested answers or completions. Select the one that BEST answers the question or completes the statement. *PRINT THE LETTER OF THE CORRECT ANSWER IN THE SPACE AT THE RIGHT.*

1. After a wedge-shaped hole has been cut into the large stone, the three-legged lifting device is inserted to lift the stone. The CORRECT order for inserting the three legs is

    A. 1, 2, 3
    B. 3, 2, 1
    C. 2, 3, 1
    D. 1, 3, 2

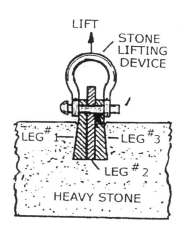

1._____

2. Brushes which have been used to apply shellac are BEST cleaned with

    A. alcohol
    C. carbon tetrachloride
    B. water
    D. acetic acid

2._____

3. When timbers are bolted together, a flat washer is GENERALLY used under the head of the bolt to

    A. prevent the bolt from turning
    B. increase the strength of the bolt
    C. reduce crushing of the wood when the bolt is tightened
    D. make it easier to turn the bolt

3._____

4. A claw hammer is PROPERLY used for

    A. driving a cold chisel
    B. driving brads
    C. setting rivets
    D. flattening a 1/4" metal bar

4._____

5. Open-end wrenches are made with the sides of the jaws at about a 15° angle to the line of the handle. This angle

    A. is useful when working the wrench in close quarters
    B. increases the strength of the jaws
    C. prevents extending the handle with a piece of pipe
    D. serves only to improve the appearance of the wrench

5._____

6. It is BEST to cut a piece of sheet metal with a pair of snips by starting each cut with the   6.____
   metal sheet

   A. out near the points of the snips
   B. as far back in the jaws as possible
   C. midway between the snip points and the pivot
   D. one-quarter the way between the snip points and the pivot

7. Cement-lined drain pipe should be cut with a   7.____

   A. chisel   B. file
   C. star drill   D. hacksaw

8. A riser is GENERALLY a pipe run which is   8.____

   A. horizontal   B. curved
   C. vertical   D. at a 45 angle

Questions 9-18.

DIRECTIONS: Questions 9 through 18 refer to the use of the tools shown below. Read the
              item, and for the operation given, select the PROPER tool to be used from
              those shown.

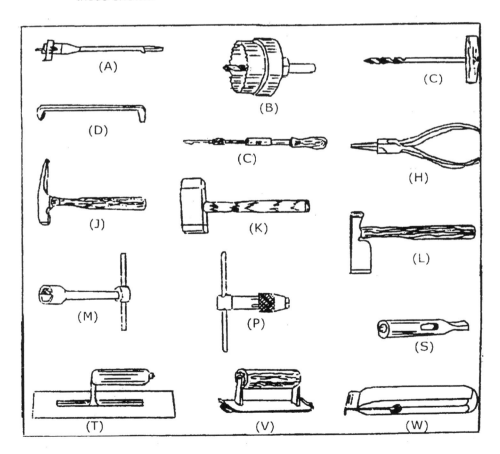

9. Turning a screw tap when threading a hole in a steel block.

9.____

10. Boring a number of different diameter holes through a heavy wood plank.

10.____

11. Quickly screwing a number of wood screws into a board.

11.____

12. Setting a groove in a cement floor before hardening of the cement.

12.____

13. Plastering a wall.

13.____

14. Chipping a small piece out of a brick to clear a projecting steel rod when building a brick wall.

14.____

15. Tightening a large nut.

15.____

16. Quickly boring a small hole through a 1/8" board.

16.____

17. Unfastening wood screws located in a position inaccessible to an ordinary screwdriver.

17.____

18. Making a 1 1/2" hole in a steel plate.

18.____

19. A pneumatic bucker is used in

19.____

    A. riveting   B. brazing
    C. soldering   D. reinforcing concrete

20. To make certain two points separated by a vertical distance of 8 feet are in perfect vertical alignment, it would be BEST to use a

20.____

    A. surface gage   B. height gage
    C. protractor   D. plumb bob

21. When repair work is being done on the elevated structure, canvas spreads are suspended under the working area MAINLY to

21.____

    A. reduce noise   B. discourage crowds
    C. protect the structure   D. protect pedestrians

22. When grinding a weld smooth, it is MOST important to avoid

22.____

    A. overheating the surrounding metal
    B. grinding too much of the weld away
    C. grinding too slowly
    D. grinding after the weld has cooled off

23. A gouge is a tool used for

23.____

    A. planing wood smooth   B. grinding metal
    C. drilling steel   D. chiseling wood

24. The tool that should be used to cut a 1" x 4" plank down to a 3" width is a

24.____

    A. hacksaw   B. crosscut saw
    C. rip saw   D. backsaw

25. Threads are cut on the ends of a length of steel pipe by the use of a

    A. brace and bit   B. counterbore
    C. stock and die   D. doweling jig

25._____

26. A bit brace can be locked so that the bit will turn in only one direction by means of a

    A. feed screw   B. rachet device
    C. universal chuck   D. ball-bearing device

26._____

27. A reamer is used to

    A. enlarge drilled holes to an exact size
    B. punch holes to desired size
    C. line up adjacent holes
    D. lay out holes before drilling

27._____

28. The tool shown at the right is a
    A. countersink
    B. counterbore
    C. star drill
    D. burring reamer

28._____

29. The saw shown at the right would be used to cut
    A. curved designs in thin wood
    B. strap iron
    C. asphalt tiles to fit against walls
    D. soft lead pipe

29._____

30. The tool shown at the right is a
    A. float
    B. finishing trowel
    C. hawk
    D. roofing seamer

30._____

KEY (CORRECT ANSWERS)

1.	D		16.	C
2.	A		17.	D
3.	C		18.	B
4.	B		19.	B
5.	A		20.	D
6.	B		21.	C
7.	D		22.	B
8.	C		23.	D
9.	P		24.	C
10.	A		25.	C
11.	E		26.	B
12.	V		27.	A
13.	T		28.	D
14.	J		29.	A
15.	M		30.	A

TEST 3

DIRECTIONS: Each question or incomplete statement is followed by several suggested answers or completions. Select the one that BEST answers the question or completes the Statement. *PRINT THE LETTER OF THE CORRECT ANSWER IN THE SPACE AT THE RIGHT.*

Questions 1-8.

DIRECTIONS: Questions 1 through 8 are to be answered on the basis of the following items. The sizes of the items shown are NOT their actual sizes. Each item is identified by a number, For each question, select the answer which gives the identifying number of the item that BEST answers the question.

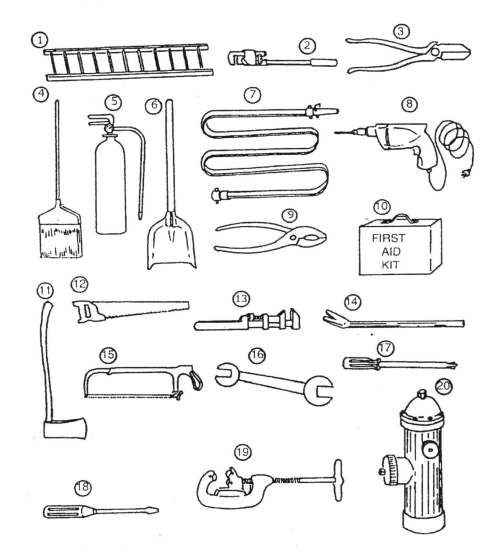

1. Which one of the following items should be connected to a hydrant and used to put out a fire?

    A. 5   B. 7   C. 8   D. 17   1._____

2. Which one of the following pairs of items should be used after a fire to clean a floor covered with small pieces of burned material?

    A. 1 and 14   B. 4 and 6   C. 10 and 12   D. 11 and 13   2._____

3. Which one of the following pairs of items should be used for cutting a branch from a tree?   3._____

    A. 2 and 3   B. 8 and 9   C. 11 and 12   D. 14 and 15

4. Which one of the following items should be used to rescue a victim from a second floor window?

    A. 1   B. 10   C. 15   D. 20   4._____

5. Which one of the following pairs of items should be used to tighten a nut on a screw?   5._____

    A. 2 and 3   B. 8 and 19   C. 9 and 14   D. 16 and 18

6. Which one of the following items should be used to repair a leaky faucet?   6._____

    A. 4   B. 5   C. 12   D. 13

7. Which one of the following items should be used as a source of water at a fire?   7._____

    A. 2   B. 6   C. 9   D. 20

8. Which item should be used for cutting metal?   8._____

    A. 6   B. 13   C. 15   D. 18

Questions 9-18.

DIRECTIONS: Questions 9 through 18, inclusive, in Column I are articles or terms used in structure maintenance and repair work, each of which is associated primarily (though not exclusively) with one of the trade specialties listed in Column II. For each article or term in Column I, select the trade specialty from Column II in which it is in greatest use. Indicate in the space at the right, the letter preceding your selected trade specialty.

COLUMN I (Articles or Terms)	COLUMN II (Trade Specialties)	
9. Drift pin	A. Carpentry	9._____
10. Studding		10._____
11. Elbow	B. Masonry	11._____
12. Header course		12._____
13. Dowel	C. Ironwork	13._____
14. Screeding		14._____
15. Cleanout	D. Plumbing	15._____
16. Air jam		16._____
17. Curing		17._____
18. Mortise and tenon		18._____

19. Practically all valves used in plumbing work are made so that the handwheel is turned clockwise instead of counterclockwise to close the valve.
The PROBABLE reason is that

    A. it is easier to remember since screws and nuts move inward when turned clock-wise
    B. the handwheel is less likely to loosen
    C. greater force can be exerted
    D. most people are righthanded

19.____

20. Sharpening a hand saw consists of

    A. jointing, shaping, setting, and filing
    B. adzing, clinching, forging, and machining
    C. brazing, chiseling, grinding, and mitering
    D. bushing, dressing, lapping, and machining

20.____

21. A hacksaw blade having 32 teeth to the inch is the BEST blade to use when cutting

    A. cold rolled steel shafting
    B. wrought iron pipe
    C. stainless steel plate
    D. copper tubing

21.____

22. Good practice dictates that an adjustable open-end wrench should be used PRIMARILY when the

    A. nut to be turned is soft and must not be scored
    B. extra leverage is needed
    C. proper size of fixed wrench is not available
    D. location is cramped permitting only a small turning angle

22.____

23. When a hacksaw blade is designated as an 18-32, the numbers 18 and 32 refer to, respectively, the blade's

    A. stroke and thickness
    B. thickness and length
    C. length and teeth per inch
    D. teeth per inch and stroke

23.____

24. When a machine screw is designated as a 10-32, the numbers 10 and 32 refer to, respectively, the screw's

    A. length and head type
    B. threads per inch and length
    C. diameter and threads per inch
    D. head type and diameter

24.____

25. An offset screwdriver is MOST useful for turning a wood screw when

    A. a strong force needs to be applied
    B. the screw head is marred
    C. space is limited
    D. speed is desired

25.____

4 (#3)

26. Of the following orders for tools or materials used in the building trades, the one which is INCOMPLETE is   26.____

    A. 1 paintbrush, flat, 2 in. wide
    B. 1 drill, twist, straight shank, high speed, 3/8 in.
    C. 1 snake, steel, 3/4 in. wide by 1/8 in. thick
    D. 1 keg of nails, 10 penny, common wire, galvanized

27. The tool that is GENERALLY used to slightly elongate a round hole in strap-iron is a   27.____

    A. rat-tail file   B. reamer
    C. drill   D. rasp

28. The BEST way to locate a point on the floor directly below a given point on the ceiling is by using a   28.____

    A. plumber's snake   B. plumb bob
    C. flashlight   D. chalk line

29. The wrench that would prove LEAST useful in uncoupling several pieces of pipe is a _____ wrench.   29.____

    A. socket   B. chain   C. strap   D. stillson

30. Of the following, the tool that is LEAST easily broken is a   30.____

    A. file   B. pry bar
    C. folding rule   D. hacksaw blade

KEY (CORRECT ANSWERS)

1.	B	16.	C
2.	B	17.	B
3.	C	18.	A
4.	A	19.	A
5.	D	20.	A
6.	D	21.	D
7.	D	22.	C
8.	C	23.	C
9.	C	24.	C
10.	A	25.	C
11.	B	26.	C
12.	D	27.	A
13.	A	28.	B
14.	B	29.	A
15.	D	30.	B

READING COMPREHENSION
UNDERSTANDING AND INTERPRETING WRITTEN MATERIAL
EXAMINATION SECTION
TEST 1

DIRECTIONS: Each question or incomplete statement is followed by several suggested answers or completions. Select the one that BEST answers the question or completes the statement. *PRINT THE LETTER OF THE CORRECT ANSWER IN THE SPACE AT THE RIGHT.*

Questions 1-2.

DIRECTIONS: Questions 1 and 2 are to be answered SOLELY on the basis of the following paragraph.

When fixing an upper sash cord, you must also remove the lower sash. To do this, the parting strip between the sash must be removed. Now remove the cover from the weight box channel, cut off the cord as before, and pull it over the pulleys. Pull your new cord over the pulleys and down into the channel where it may be fastened to the weight. The cord for an upper sash is cut off 1" or 2" below the pulley with the weight resting on the floor of the pocket and the cord held taut. These measurements allow for slight stretching of the cord. When the cord is cut to length, it can be pulled up over the pulley and tied with a single common knot in the end to fit into the socket in the sash groove. If the knot protrudes beyond the face of the sash, tap it gently to flatten. In this way, it will not become frayed from constant rubbing against the groove.

1. When repairing the upper sash cord, the FIRST thing to do is to   1._____
    A. remove the lower sash
    B. cut the existing sash cord
    C. remove the parting strip
    D. measure the length of new cord necessary

2. According to the above paragraph, the rope may become frayed if the   2._____
    A. pulley is too small   B. knot sticks out
    C. cord is too long   D. weight is too heavy

Questions 3-4.

DIRECTIONS: Questions 3 and 4 are to be answered SOLELY on the basis of the following paragraph.

Repeated burning of the same area should be avoided. Burning should not be done on impervious, shallow, unstable, or highly erodible soils, or on steep slopes—especially in areas subject to heavy rains or rapid snowmelt. When existing vegetation is likely to be killed or seriously weakened by the fire, measures should be taken to assure prompt revegetation of the burned area. Burns should be limited to relatively small proportions of a watershed unit so that the stream channels will be able to carry any increased flows with a minimum of damage.

3. According to the above paragraph, planned burning should be limited to small areas of the watershed because
 A. the fire can be better controlled
 B. existing vegetation will be less likely to be killed
 C. plants will grow quicker in small areas
 D. there will be less likelihood of damaging floods

3._____

4. According to the above paragraph, burning USUALLY should be done on soils that
 A. readily absorb moisture
 B. have been burnt before
 C. exist as a thin layer over rock
 D. can be flooded by nearby streams

4._____

Questions 5-11.

DIRECTIONS: Questions 5 through 11 are to be answered SOLELY on the basis of the following paragraph.

FUSE INFORMATION

 Badly bent or distorted fuse clips cannot be permitted. Sometimes, the distortion or bending is so slight that it escapes notice, yet it may be the cause for fuse failures through the heat that is developed by the poor contact. Occasionally, the proper spring tension of the fuse clips has been destroyed by overheating from loose wire connections to the clips. Proper contact surfaces must be maintained to avoid faulty operation of the fuse. Maintenance men should remove oxides that form on the copper and brass contacts, check the clip pressure, and make sure that contact surfaces are not deformed or bent in any way. When removing oxides, use a well-worn file and remove only the oxide film. Do not use sandpaper or emery cloth as hard particles may come off and become embedded in the contact surfaces. All wire connections to the fuse holders should be carefully inspected to see that they are tight.

5. Fuse failure because of poor clip contact or loose connections is due to the resulting
 A. excessive voltage B. increased current
 C. lowered resistance D. heating effect

5._____

6. Oxides should be removed from fuse contacts by using
 A. a dull file B. emery cloth
 C. fine sandpaper D. a sharp file

6._____

7. One result of loose wire connections at the terminal of a fuse clip is stated in the above paragraph to be
 A. loss of tension in the wire
 B. welding of the fuse to the clip
 C. distortion of the clip
 D. loss of tension of the clip

7._____

8. Simple reasoning will show that the oxide film referred to is undesirable CHIEFLY because it
   A. looks dull
   B. makes removal of the fuse difficult
   C. weakens the clips
   D. introduces undesirable resistance

8._____

9. Fuse clips that are bent very slightly
   A. should be replaced with new clips
   B. should be carefully filed
   C. may result in blowing of the fuse
   D. may prevent the fuse from blowing

9._____

10. From the fuse information paragraph, it would be reasonable to conclude that fuse clips
    A. are difficult to maintain
    B. must be given proper maintenance
    C. require more attention than other electrical equipment
    D. are unreliable

10._____

11. A safe practical way of checking the tightness of the wire connection to the fuse clips of a live 120-volt lighting circuit is to
    A. feel the connection with your hand to see if it is warm
    B. try tightening with an insulated screwdriver or socket wrench
    C. see if the circuit works
    D. measure the resistance with an ohmmeter

11._____

Questions 12-13.

DIRECTIONS: Questions 12 through 13 are to be answered SOLELY on the basis of the following paragraph.

For cast iron pipe lines, the middle ring or sleeve shall have *beveled* ends and shall be high quality cast iron. The middle ring shall have a minimum wall thickness of 3/8" for pipe up to 8", 7/16" for pipe 10" to 30", and 1/2" for pipe over 30", nominal diameter. Minimum length of middle ring shall be 5" for pipe up to 10", 6" for pipe 10" to 30", and 10" for pipe 30" nominal diameter and larger. The middle ring shall not have a center pipe stop, unless otherwise specified.

12. As used in the above paragraph, the word *beveled* means MOST NEARLY
    A. straight   B. slanted   C. curved   D. rounded

12._____

13. In accordance with the above paragraph, the middle ring of a 24" nominal diameter pipe would have a minimum wall thickness and length of _____ thick and _____ long.
    A. 3/8"; 5:   B. 3/8"; 6"
    C. 7/16"; 6"   D. 1/2"; 6"

13._____

Questions 14-17.

DIRECTIONS: Questions 14 through 17 are to be answered SOLELY on the basis of the following paragraph.

Operators spotting loads with long booms and working around men need the smooth, easy operation and positive control of uniform pressure swing clutches. There are no jerks or grabs with these large disc-type clutches because there is always even pressure over the entire clutch lining surface. In the conventional band-type swing clutch, the pressure varies between dead and live ends of the band. The uniform pressure swing clutch has excellent provision for heat dissipation. The driving elements, which are always rotating, have a great number of fins cast in them. This gives them an impeller or blower action for cooling, resulting in longer life and freedom from frequent adjustment.

14. According to the above paragraph, it may be said that conventional band-type swing clutches have   14._____
    A.   even pressure on the clutch lining
    B.   larger contact area
    C.   smaller contact area
    D.   uneven pressure on the clutch lining

15. According to the above paragraph, machines equipped with uniform pressure swing clutches will   15._____
    A.   give better service under all conditions
    B.   require no clutch adjustment
    C.   give positive control of hoist
    D.   provide better control of swing

16. According to the above paragraph, it may be said that the rotation of the driving elements of the uniform pressure swing clutch is ALWAYS   16._____
    A.   continuous   B.   constant
    C.   varying   D.   uncertain

17. According to the above paragraph, freedom from frequent adjustment is due to the   17._____
    A.   operator's smooth, easy operation
    B.   positive control of the clutch
    C.   cooling effect of the rotating fins
    D.   larger contact area of the bigger clutch

Questions 18-22.

DIRECTIONS: Questions 18 through 22 are to be answered SOLELY on the basis of the following paragraphs.

Exhaust valve clearance adjustment on diesel engines is very important for proper operation of the engine. Insufficient clearance between the exhaust valve stem and the rocker arm causes a loss of compression and, after a while, burning of the valves and valve seat inserts. On the other hand, too much valve clearance will result in noisy operation of the engine.

Exhaust valves that are maintained in good operating condition will result in efficient combustion in the engine. Valve seats must be true and unpitted, and valve stems must work smoothly within the valve guides. Long valve life will result from proper maintenance and operation of the engine.

Engine operating temperatures should be maintained between 160°F and 185°F. Low operating temperatures result in incomplete combustion and the deposit of fuel lacquers on valves.

18. According to the above paragraphs, too much valve clearance will cause the engine to operate
    A. slowly   B. noisily   C. smoothly   D. cold

18._____

19. On the basis of the information given in the above paragraphs, operating temperatures of a diesel engine should be between
    A. 125°F and 130°F   B. 140°F and 150°F
    C. 160°F and 185°F   D. 190°F and 205°F

19._____

20. According to the above paragraphs, the deposit of fuel lacquers on valves is caused by
    A. high operating temperatures
    B. insufficient valve clearance
    C. low operating temperatures
    D. efficient combustion

20._____

21. According to the above paragraphs, for efficient operation of the engine, valve seats must
    A. have sufficient clearance
    B. be true and unpitted
    C. operate at low temperatures
    D. be adjusted regularly

21._____

22. According to the above paragraphs, a loss of compression is due to insufficient clearance between the exhaust valve stem and the
    A. rocker arm   B. valve seat
    C. valve seat inserts   D. valve guides

22._____

Questions 23-25.

DIRECTIONS: Questions 23 through 25 are to be answered SOLELY on the basis of the following excerpt:

A SPECIFICATION FOR ELECTRIC WORK FOR THE CITY

Breakers shall be equipped with magnetic blowout coils...Handles of breakers shall be trip-free...Breakers shall be designed to carry 100% of trip rating continuously; to have inverse time delay tripping above 100% of trip rating...

23. According to the above paragraph, the breaker shall have provision for
    A. resetting   B. arc quenching
    C. adjusting trip time   D. adjusting trip rating

23._____

24. According to the above paragraph, the breaker
    A. shall trip easily at exactly 100% of trip rating
    B. shall trip instantly at a little more than 100% of trip rating
    C. should be constructed so that it shall not be possible to prevent it from opening on overload or short circuit by holding the handle in the ON position
    D. shall not trip prematurely at 100% of trip rating

24._____

25. According to the above paragraph, the breaker shall trip   25._____
    A. instantaneously as soon as 100% of trip rating is reached
    B. instantaneously as soon as 100% of trip rating is exceeded
    C. more quickly the greater the current, once 100% of trip rating is exceeded
    D. after a predetermined fixed time lapse, once 100% of trip rating is reached

_____

KEY (CORRECT ANSWERS)

1.	C		11.	B
2.	B		12.	B
3.	D		13.	C
4.	A		14.	D
5.	D		15.	D
6.	A		16.	A
7.	D		17.	C
8.	D		18.	B
9.	C		19.	C
10.	B		20.	C

21.	B
22.	A
23.	B
24.	C
25.	C

_____

TEST 2

DIRECTIONS: Each question or incomplete statement is followed by several suggested answers or completions. Select the one that BEST answers the question or completes the statement. *PRINT THE LETTER OF THE CORRECT ANSWER IN THE SPACE AT THE RIGHT.*

Questions 1-4.

DIRECTIONS: Questions 1 through 4 are to be answered SOLELY on the basis of the following paragraph.

A low pressure hot water boiler shall include a relief valve or valves of a capacity such that with the heat generating equipment operating at maximum, the pressure cannot rise more than 20 percent above the maximum allowable working pressure (set pressure) if that is 30 p.s.i. gage or less, nor more than 10 percent if it is more than 30 p.s.i. gage. The difference between the set pressure and the pressure at which the valve is relieving is known as *over-pressure or accumulation*. If the steam relieving capacity in pounds per hour is calculated, it shall be determined by dividing by 1,000 the maximum BTU output at the boiler nozzle obtainable from the heat generating equipment, or by multiplying the square feet of heating surface by five.

1. In accordance with the above paragraph, the capacity of a relief valve should be computed on the basis of
   A. size of boiler
   B. maximum rated capacity of generating equipment
   C. average output of the generating equipment
   D. minimum capacity of generating equipment

   1._____

2. In accordance with the above paragraph, with a set pressure of 30 p.s.i. gage, the overpressure should not be more than _____ p.s.i.
   A. 3   B. 6   C. 33   D. 36

   2._____

3. In accordance with the above paragraph, a relief valve should start relieving at a pressure equal to the
   A. set pressure
   B. over pressure
   C. over pressure minus set pressure
   D. set pressure plus over pressure

   3._____

4. In accordance with the above paragraph, the steam relieving capacity can be computed by
   A. *multiplying* the maximum BTU output by 5
   B. *dividing* the pounds of steam per hour by 1,000
   C. *dividing* the maximum BTU output by the square feet of heating surface
   D. *dividing* the maximum BTU output by 1,000

   4._____

Questions 5-8.

DIRECTIONS: Questions 5 through 8 are to be answered SOLELY on the basis of the following paragraph.

Air conditioning units requiring a minimum rate of flow of water in excess of one-half (1/2) gallon per minute shall be metered. Air conditioning equipment with a refrigeration unit which has a definite rate of capacity in tons or fractions thereof, the charge will be at the rate of $30 per annum per ton capacity from the date installed to the date when the supply is metered. Such units, when equipped with an approved water-conserving device, shall be charged at the rate of $4.50 per annum per ton capacity from the date installed to the date when the supply is metered.

5. A man who was in the market for air conditioning equipment was considering three different units. Unit 1 required a flow of 28 gallons of water per hour; Unit 2 required 30 gallons of water per hour; Unit 3 required 32 gallons of water per hour. The man asked the salesman which units would require the installation of a water meter. According to the above passage, the salesman SHOULD answer: 5._____
    A. All three units require meters
    B. Units 2 and 3 require meters
    C. Unit 3 only requires a meter
    D. None of the units require a meter

6. Suppose that air conditioning equipment with a refrigeration unit of 10 tons was put in operation on October 1; and in the following year on July 1, a meter was installed. According to the above passage, the charge for this period would be _____ the annual rate. 6._____
    A. twice   B. equal to
    C. three-fourths   D. one-fourth

7. The charge for air conditioning equipment which has no refrigeration unit 7._____
    A. is $30 per year
    B. is $25.50 per year
    C. is $4.50 per year
    D. cannot be determined from the above passage

8. The charge for air conditioning equipment with a seven-ton refrigeration unit equipped with an approved water-conserving device 8._____
    A. is $4.50 per year
    B. is $25.50 per year
    C. is $31.50 per year
    D. cannot be determined from the above passage

Questions 9-14.

DIRECTIONS: Questions 9 through 14 are to be answered SOLELY on the basis of the following paragraph.

The city makes unremitting efforts to keep the water free from pollution. An inspectional force under a sanitary expert is engaged in patrolling the watersheds to see that the department's sanitary regulations are observed. Samples taken daily from various points in the water supply system are examined and analyzed at the three laboratories maintained by the department. All water before delivery to the distribution mains is treated with chlorine to destroy bacteria. In addition, some water is aerated to free it from gases and, in some cases, from microscopic organisms. Generally, microscopic organisms which develop in the reservoirs and at times impart an unpleasant taste and odor to the water, though in no sense harmful to health, are destroyed by treatment with copper sulfate and by chlorine dosage. None of the supplies is filtered, but the quality of the water supplied by the city is excellent for all purposes, and it is clear and wholesome.

9. According to the above paragraph, microscopic organisms are removed from the water supplied to the city by means of   9._____
    A.   chlorine alone
    B.   chlorine, aeration, and filtration
    C.   chlorine, aeration, filtration, and sampling
    D.   copper sulfate, chlorine, and aeration

10. Microscopic organisms in the water supply GENERALLY are   10._____
    A.   a health menace   B.   impossible to detect
    C.   not harmful to health   D.   not destroyed in the water

11. The MAIN function of the inspectional force, as described in the above paragraph, is to   11._____
    A.   take samples of water for analysis
    B.   enforce sanitary regulations
    C.   add chlorine to the water supply
    D.   inspect water-use meters

12. According to the above paragraph, chlorine is added to water before entering the   12._____
    A.   watersheds   B.   reservoirs
    C.   distribution mains   D.   run-off areas

13. Of the following suggested headings or titles for the above paragraph, the one that BEST tells what the paragraph is about is   13._____
    A.   QUALITY OF WATER   B.   CHLORINATION OF WATER
    C.   TESTING OF WATER   D.   BACTERIA IN WATER

14. The MOST likely reason for taking samples of water for examination and analysis from various points in the water supply system is: 14._____
    A.   The testing points are convenient to the department's laboratories
    B.   Water from one part of the system may be made undrinkable by a local condition
    C.   The samples can be distributed equally among the three laboratories
    D.   The hardness or softness of water varies from place to place

Questions 15-17.

DIRECTIONS: Questions 15 through 17 are to be answered SOLELY on the basis of the following paragraph.

    A building measuring 200' x 100' at the street is set back 20' on all sides at the 15th floor, and an additional 10' on all sides at the 30th floor. The building is 35 stories high.

15. The **floor** area of the 16th floor is MOST NEARLY _____ sq. ft. 15._____
    A. 20,000   B. 14,400   C. 9,600   D. 7,500

16. The floor area of the 35th floor is MOST NEARLY _____ sq. ft. 16._____
    A. 20,000   B. 13,900   C. 7,500   D. 5,600

17. The floor area of the 16th floor, compared to the floor area of the 2nd floor, is 17._____
    MOST NEARLY _____ as much.
    A. three-fourths (3/4)   B. two-thirds (2/3)
    C. one-half (1/2)   D. four-tenths (4/10)

Question 18.

DIRECTIONS: Question 18 is to be answered SOLELY on the basis of the following
               paragraph.

Experience has shown that, in general, a result of the installation of meters on
services not previously metered is to reduce the amount of water consumed, but is not
necessarily to reduce the peak load on plumbing systems. The permissible head loss
through meters at their rated maximum flow is 20 p.s.i. The installation of a meter may
therefore appreciably lower the pressures available in fixtures on a plumbing system.

18. According to the above paragraph, a water meter may 18._____
    A. limit the flow in the plumbing system of 20 p.s.i.
    B. reduce the peak load on the plumbing system
    C. increase the overall amount of water consumed
    D. reduce the pressure in the plumbing system

Question 19.

DIRECTIONS: Question 19 is to be answered SOLELY on the basis of the following
               paragraph.

Spring comes without trumpets to a city. The asphalt is a wilderness that does
not quicken overnight; winds blow gritty with cinders instead of merry with the smells of
earth and fertilizer. Women wear their gardens on their hats. But spring is a season in
the city, and it has its own harbingers, constant as daffodils. Shop windows change
their colors, people walk more slowly on the streets, what one can see of the sky has a
bluer tone. Pulitzer prizes awake and sing and matinee tickets go-a-begging. But gayer
than any of these are the carousels, which are already in sheltered places, beginning to
turn with the sound of springtime itself. They are the earliest and the truest and the
oldest of all the urban signs.

19. In the passage above, the word *harbingers* means 19._____
    A. storms   B. truths   C. virtues   D. forerunners

Questions 20-22.

DIRECTIONS: Questions 20 through 22 are to be answered SOLELY on the basis
               of the following paragraph.

Gas heaters include manually operated, automatic, and instantaneous heaters. Some heaters are equipped with a thermostat which controls the fuel supply so that when the water falls below a predetermined temperature, the fuel is automatically turned on. In some types, the hot-water storage tank is well-insulated to economize the use of fuel. Instantaneous heaters are arranged so that the opening of a faucet on the hot-water pipe will increase the flow of fuel, which is ignited by a continuously burning pilot light to heat the water to from 120° to 130°F. The possibility that the pilot light will die out offers a source of danger in the use of automatic appliances which depend on a pilot light. Gas and oil heaters are dangerous, and they should be designed to prevent the accumulation, in a confined space within the heater, of a large volume of an explosive mixture.

20. According to the above passage, the opening of a hot-water faucet on a hot-water pipe connected to an instantaneous hot-water heater will ____ the pilot light.
    A. *increase* the temperature of
    B. *increase* the flow of fuel to
    C. *decrease* the flow of fuel to
    D. *have a marked effect* on

20._____

21. According to the above passage, the fuel is automatically turned on in a heater equipped with a thermostat whenever
    A. the water temperature drops below 120°F
    B. the pilot light is lit
    C. the water temperature drops below some predetermined temperature
    D. a hot water supply is opened

21._____

22. According to the above passage, some hot-water storage tanks are well-insulated to
    A. accelerate the burning of the fuel
    B. maintain the water temperature between 120° and 130°F
    C. prevent the pilot light from being extinguished
    D. minimize the expenditure of fuel

22._____

Question 23.

DIRECTIONS: Question 23 is to be answered SOLELY on the basis of the following paragraph.

Breakage of the piston under high-speed operation has been the commonest fault of disc piston meters. Various techniques are adopted to prevent this, such as *throttling* the meter, cutting away the edge of the piston, or reinforcing it, but these are simply makeshifts.

23. As used in the above paragraph, the word *throttling* means MOST NEARLY
    A. enlarging   B. choking
    C. harnessing   D. dismantling

23._____

Questions 24-25.

DIRECTIONS: Questions 24 and 25 are to be answered SOLELY on the basis of the following paragraph.

One of the most common and objectionable difficulties occurring in a drainage system is trap seal loss. This failure can be attributed directly to inadequate ventilation of the trap and the subsequent negative and positive pressures which occur. A trap seal may be lost either by siphonage and/or back pressure. Loss of the trap seal by siphonage is the result of a negative pressure in the drainage system. The seal content of the trap is forced by siphonage into the waste piping of the drainage system through exertion of atmospheric pressure on the fixture side of the trap seal.

24. According to the above paragraph, a positive pressure is a direct result of   24._____
   A. siphonage   B. unbalanced trap seal
   C. poor ventilation   D. atmospheric pressure

25. According to the above paragraph, the water in the trap is forced into the drain   25._____
   pipe by
   A. atmospheric pressure   B. back pressure
   C. negative pressure   D. back pressure on fixture side of seal

KEY (CORRECT ANSWERS)

1.	B		11.	B
2.	B		12.	C
3.	D		13.	A
4.	D		14.	B
5.	C		15.	C
6.	C		16.	D
7.	D		17.	C
8.	C		18.	D
9.	D		19.	B
10.	C		20.	B

21.	C
22.	D
23.	B
24.	C
25.	A

READING COMPREHENSION
UNDERSTANDING AND INTERPRETING WRITTEN MATERIAL
EXAMINATION SECTION
TEST 1

DIRECTIONS: Each question or incomplete statement is followed by several suggested answers or completions. Select the one that BEST answers the question or completes the statement. *PRINT THE LETTER OF THE CORRECT ANSWER IN THE SPACE AT THE RIGHT.*

Questions 1-5.

DIRECTIONS: Questions 1 through 5 are to be answered SOLELY on the basis of the following paragraph.

The strength of the seal of a trap is closely proportional to the depth of the seal, regardless of the size of the trap. Unfortunately, an increase in the depth of the seal also increases the probability of solids being retained in the trap, and a limit of about a 4" depth of seal for traps that must pass solids has been imposed by some plumbing codes. The depth of seal most commonly found in simple traps is between $1\frac{1}{2}$" and 2". The Hoover Report recommends a minimum depth of 2" as a safeguard against seal rupture and a maximum depth of 4" to avoid clogging, fungus growths, and similar difficulties. Traps in rain-water leaders and other pipes carrying clear-water wastes only, and which are infrequently used, should have seal depths equal to or greater than 4". The increase in the volume of water retained in the trap helps very little in increasing the strength of the seal, but it does materially reduce the velocity of flow through the trap so as to increase the probability of the sedimentation of solids therein.

1. In accordance with the above, it may be said that traps carrying rain-water should have a seal of

    A. 5"
    B. $3\frac{1}{2}$"
    C. 2"
    D. $1\frac{1}{2}$"

1._____

2. In accordance with the preceding paragraph, which one of the following statements is MOST NEARLY correct?

    A. Simple traps have a depth of seal between $1\frac{1}{2}$" to 4".
    B. A minimum depth of 4" is recommended to avoid seal rupture.
    C. The strength of the seal is proportional to the size of the trap.
    D. The higher the depth of seal, the more chance of collecting solids.

2._____

3. In accordance with the above, it may be said that increasing the volume of water retained   3._____
   in a trap may

   A. *greatly* increase the velocity of flow
   B. *slightly* increase the velocity of flow
   C. *greatly* increase the trap seal
   D. *slightly* increase the trap seal

4. Of the following, the title which BEST explains the main idea of this paragraph is   4._____

   A. TRAP SEAL DEPTHS
   B. THE EFFECTS OF SEDIMENTATION ON TRAP SEALS
   C. COMMON TRAP SIZES
   D. TRAP SIZES AND VELOCITY OF FLOW

5. Assume that the strength of a trap seal is indicated by 8 units when the trap depth is 2".   5._____
   In accordance with the above paragraph, increasing the depth of seal to 4" will cause
   the strength of the trap seal to be MOST NEARLY _____ units.

   A. 2   B. 4   C. 8   D. 16

Questions 6-10.

DIRECTIONS: Questions 6 through 10 are to be answered SOLELY on the basis of the follow-
               ing paragraph.

The thickness of insulation necessary for the most economical results varies with the
steam temperature. The standard covering consists of 85 percent magnesia with 10 percent of
long-fibre asbestos as a binder. Both magnesia and laminated asbestos—felt and other forms of
mineral wool including glass wool—are also used for heat insulation. The magnesia and laminated asbestos coverings may be safely used at temperatures up to 600° F. Pipe insulation is
applied in molded sections 3 feet long. The sections are attached to the pipe by means of galvanized iron wire or netting. Flanges and fittings can be insulated by direct application of magnesia cement to the metal without reinforcement. Insulation should always be maintained in
good condition because it saves fuel. Routine maintenance of warm-pipe insulation should
include prompt repair of damaged surfaces. Steam and hot water leaks concealed by insulation
will be difficult to detect. Underground steam or hotwater pipes are best insulated using a concrete trench with removable cover.

6. The word *reinforcement,* as used above, means MOST NEARLY   6._____

   A. resistance   B. strengthening
   C. regulation   D. removal

7. According to the above paragraph, magnesia and laminated-asbestos coverings may be   7._____
   safely used at temperatures up to

   A. 800° F   B. 720° F   C. 675° F   D. 600° F

8. According to the above paragraph, insulation should ALWAYS be maintained in good   8._____
   condition because it

   A. is laminated   B. saves fuel
   C. is attached to the pipe   D. prevents leaks

9. According to the above paragraph, pipe insulation sections are attached to the pipe by means of

    A. binders
    C. netting
    B. mineral wool
    D. staples

9._____

10. According to the above paragraph, a leak in a hot-water pipe may be difficult to detect because when insulation is used, the leak is

    A. underground
    C. routine
    B. hidden
    D. cemented

10._____

Questions 11-15.

DIRECTIONS: Questions 11 through 15 are to be answered SOLELY on the basis of the following paragraph.

Reductions in pipe size of a building heating system are made with eccentric fittings and are pitched downward. The ends of mains with gravity return shall be at least 18" above the water line of the boiler. As condensate flows opposite to the stream, runouts are one size larger than the vertical pipe and are pitched upward. In a one-pipe system, an automatic air vent must be provided at each main to relieve air pressure and to let steam enter the radiator. As steam enters the radiator, a thermal device causes the vent to close, thereby holding the steam. Steam mains should not be less than two inches in diameter. The end of the steam main should have a minimum size of one-half of its greatest diameter. Small steam systems should be sized for a 2 oz. pressure drop. Large steam systems should be sized for a 4 oz. pressure drop.

11. The word *thermal,* as used in the above paragraph, means MOST NEARLY

    A. convector   B. heat   C. instrument   D. current

11._____

12. According to the above paragraph, the one of the following that is one size larger than the vertical pipe is the

    A. steam main
    C. water line
    B. valve
    D. runout

12._____

13. According to the above paragraph, small steam systems should be sized for a pressure drop of _____ ounces.

    A. 2   B. 3   C. 4   D. 5

13._____

14. According to the above paragraph, ends of mains with gravity return shall be AT LEAST

    A. 18" above the water line of the boiler
    B. one-quarter of the greatest diameter of the main
    C. twice the size of the vertical pipe in the main
    D. 18" above the steam line of the boiler

14._____

15. According to the above paragraph, the one of the following that is provided at each main to relieve air pressure is a(n)

    A. gravity return
    C. eccentric
    B. convector
    D. vent

15._____

Questions 16-17.

DIRECTIONS: Questions 16 and 17 are to be answered SOLELY on the basis of the following paragraph.

In determining the size of a storm drain, a number of factors must be taken into consideration. One factor which makes sizing the storm drain difficult is the matter of predicting rainfall over a given period. Using a maximum estimate of about 1 inch of rain in a 10-minute interval, the approximate volume of water that will fall on a roof or surface in one minute's time can be determined readily. Another factor is the pitch and material of a roof or surface upon which the rain falls. A surface that has a pitch and smooth surface would increase the flow of water into a drain pipe.

16. According to the above paragraph, the statement which includes all factors needed to determine the size of a drain pipe is the   16._____

    A. maximum rainfall on a surface
    B. pitch and surface of the area
    C. amount of water to be piped in a definite time interval
    D. area of the surface

17. A roof that has a 45° pitch would PROBABLY have a drain pipe size   17._____

    A. smaller than a roof with no pitch
    B. larger than a roof with no pitch
    C. equal to that of a flat roof
    D. equal to the amount of water falling in ten minutes

Questions 18-19.

DIRECTIONS: Questions 18 and 19 are to be answered SOLELY on the basis of the following paragraph.

Because of the large capacity of unit heaters, care should be taken to see that the steam piping leading to them is of sufficient size. Unit heaters should not be used on one-pipe systems. If the heating system contains direct radiators operated with steam under vacuum, it is best to have the unit heaters served by a separate main so that steam above atmospheric pressure can be supplied to the units, if desired, without interfering with the operation of the direct radiators.

18. According to the above paragraph, unit heaters are supplied with   18._____

    A. steam under vacuum
    B. steam from direct radiators
    C. separate steam lines
    D. steam preferably from a one-pipe system

19. According to the above paragraph, it may be said that unit heaters work BEST with   19._____

    A. steam above atmospheric pressure   B. direct radiators
    C. one-pipe system   D. vacuum systems

Questions 20-21.

DIRECTIONS: Questions 20 and 21 are to be answered SOLELY on the basis of the following paragraph.

Most heating units emit heat by radiation and convection. An exposed radiator emits approximately half of its heat by radiation, the amount depending upon the size and number of sections. In general, a thin radiator, such as a wall radiator, emits a larger proportion of its heat by radiation than does a thick radiator. When a radiator is enclosed or shielded, the proportion of heat emitted by radiation is reduced. The balance of the emission occurs by conduction to the air in contact with the heating surface, and this heated air rises by circulation due to convection and transmits this warm air to the space which is to be heated.

20.   According to the above paragraph, when a radiator is enclosed, a GREATER portion of the heat is emitted to the room by   20._____

    A.   convection   B.   radiation
    C.   conduction   D.   transmission

21.   According to the above paragraph, the amount of heat that a radiator emits is   21._____

    A.   approximately half of its heat by radiation
    B.   determined by the thickness of the radiator
    C.   dependent upon whether it is exposed or enclosed
    D.   dependent upon the size and number of sections of the radiator

Questions 22-25.

DIRECTIONS: Questions 22 through 25 are to be answered SOLELY on the basis of the following paragraph.

Safety valves are required to operate without chattering and to be set to close after blowing down not more than 4% of the set pressure, but not less than 2 lbs. in any case. For pressure between 100 and 300 lbs., inclusive, the blow down is required to be not less than 2% of the set pressure. The blow down adjustment is made and sealed by the manufacturer. The popping-point tolerance plus or minus is required not to exceed 2 lbs. for pressure up to and including 70 lbs., 3 lbs. for pressure 71 to 300 lbs., and 10 lbs. for pressure over 300 lbs.

22.   A boiler is being installed to operate at a maximum allowable pressure of 10 lb., and the safety valve has been set to blow at this pressure.   22._____
This valve should close after the boiler blows down to NOT MORE THAN _____ lb.

    A.   9.6   B.   4.0   C.   9.8   D.   8.0

23.   A boiler is being installed to operate at a maximum allowable working pressure of 300 lb., and the safety valve is set to blow at this pressure. This valve should close after the boiler blows down to NOT MORE THAN _____ lb.   23._____

    A.   204   B.   298   C.   12   D.   6

24. A sealed safety valve is to be installed on a superheater header in a power steam gener- 24._____
ating plant. The marking on this valve shows that it is set to pop at 425 lb.
This valve would operate satisfactorily if it popped at EITHER _____ or _____ lb.

    A.   425; 445   B.   415; 435
    C.   372.5; 467.5   D.   412.25; 437.75

25. A sealed safety valve is to be installed on a boiler in a high pressure steam generating 25._____
station. The marking on the valve shows that it is set to pop at 300 lb.
This valve would operate satisfactorily if it popped at EITHER _____ or _____ lb.

    A.   290; 310   B.   297; 303
    C.   291; 309   D.   288; 312

_____

KEY (CORRECT ANSWERS)

1. A		11. B
2. D		12. D
3. D		13. A
4. A		14. A
5. D		15. D
6. B		16. C
7. D		17. B
8. B		18. C
9. C		19. A
10. B		20. A

21. D
22. D
23. A
24. B
25. B

_____

TEST 2

Questions 1-6.

DIRECTIONS: Questions 1 through 6 are to be answered SOLELY on the basis of the following paragraph.

FIRST AID INSTRUCTIONS

The main purpose of first aid is to put the injured person in the best possible position until medical help arrives. This includes the performance of emergency treatment for the purpose of saving a life if a doctor is not present. When a person is hurt, a crowd usually gathers around the victim. If nobody uses his head, the injured person fails to get the care he needs. You must stay calm and, most important, it is your duty to take charge at an accident. The first thing for you to do is to see, as best you can, what is wrong with the injured person. Leave the victim where he is until the nature and extent of his injury are determined. If he is unconscious, he should not be moved, except to lay him flat on his back if he is in some other position. Loosen the clothing of any seriously hurt person, and make him as comfortable as possible. Medical help should be called as soon as possible. You should remain with the injured person and send someone else to call the doctor. You should try to make sure that the one who calls for a doctor is able to give correct information as to the location of the injured person. In order to help the physician to know what equipment may be needed in each particular case, the person making the call should give the doctor as much information about the injury as possible.

1. If nobody uses his head at the scene of an accident, there is danger that   1.____

   A. no one will get the names of all the witnesses
   B. a large crowd will gather
   C. the victim will not get the care he needs
   D. the victim will blame the city for negligence

2. When an accident occurs, the FIRST thing you should do is   2.____

   A. call a doctor
   B. loosen the clothing of the injured person
   C. notify the victim's family
   D. try to find out what is wrong with the injured person

3. If you do NOT know the extent and nature of the victim's injuries, you should   3.____

   A. let the injured person lie where he is
   B. immediately take the victim to a hospital yourself
   C. help the injured person to his feet to see if he can walk
   D. have the injured person sit up on the ground while you examine him

4. If the injured person is breathing and unconscious, you should 4._____

    A. get some hot liquid such as coffee or tea into him
    B. give him artificial respiration
    C. lift up his head to try to stimulate blood circulation
    D. see that he lies flat on his back

5. If it is necessary to call a doctor, you should 5._____

    A. go and make the call yourself since you have all the information
    B. find out who the victim's family doctor is before making the call
    C. have someone else make the call who know the location of the victim
    D. find out which doctor the victim can afford

6. It is important for the caller to give the doctor as much information as is available regard- 6._____
ing the injury so that the doctor

    A. can bring the necessary equipment
    B. can make out an accident report
    C. will be responsible for any malpractice resulting from the first aid treatment
    D. can inform his nurse on how long he will be in the field

Questions 7-8.

DIRECTIONS: Questions 7 and 8 are to be answered SOLELY on the basis of the following
                paragraph.

PRECIPITATION AND RUNOFF

In the United States, the average annual precipitation is about 30 inches, of which about 21 inches is lost to the atmosphere by evaporation and transpiration. The remaining 9 inches becomes runoff into rivers and lakes. Both the precipitation and runoff vary greatly with geography and season. Annual precipitation varies from more than 100 inches in parts of the northwest to only 2 or 3 inches in parts of the southwest. In the northeastern part of the country, including New York State, the annual average precipitation is about 45 inches, of which about 22 inches becomes runoff. Even in New York State, there is some variation from place to place and considerable variation from time to time. During extremely dry years, the precipitation may be as low as 30 inches and the runoff below 10 inches. In general, there are greater variations in runoff rates from smaller watersheds. A critical water supply situation occurs when there are three or four abnormally dry years in succession.

Precipitation over the state is measured and recorded by a network of stations operated by the U.S. Weather Bureau. All of the precipitation records and other data such as temperature, humidity, and evaporation rates are published monthly by the Weather Bureau in *Climatological Data*. Runoff rates at more than 200 stream-gauging stations in the state are measured and recorded by the U.S. Geological Survey in cooperation with various state agencies. Records of the daily average flows are published annually by the U.S. Geological Survey in *Surface Water Records of New York*. Copies may be obtained by writing to the Water Resources Division, United States Geological Survey, Albany, New York 23301.

7. From the above paragraphs, it is APPROPRIATE to conclude that   7.____

    A. critical supply situations do not occur
    B. the greater the rainfall, the greater the runoff
    C. there are greater variations in runoff from larger watersheds
    D. the rainfall in the southwest is greater than the average in the country

8. From the above paragraphs, it is APPROPRIATE to conclude that   8.____

    A. an annual rainfall of about 50 inches does not occur in New York State
    B. the U.S. Weather Bureau is only interested in rainfall
    C. runoff is equal to rainfall less losses to the atmosphere
    D. information about rainfall and runoff in New York State is unavailable to the public

Questions 9-10.

DIRECTIONS: Questions 9 through 10 are to be answered SOLELY on the basis of the following paragraph.

NATURAL LAKES

Large lakes may yield water of exceptionally fine quality except near the shore line and in the vicinity of sewer outlets or near outlets of large streams. Therefore, minimum treatment is required. The availability of practically unlimited quantities of water is also a decided advantage. Unfortunately, however, the sewage from a city is often discharged into the same lake from which the water supply is taken. Great care must be taken in locating both the water intake and the sewer outlet so that the pollution handled by the water treatment plant is a minimum.

Sometimes the distance from the shore where dependable, satisfactory water can be found is so great that the cost of water intake facilities is prohibitive for a small municipality. In such cases, another supply must be found, or water must be obtained from a neigh-boring large city. Lake water is usually uniform in quality from day to day and does not vary in temperature as much as water from a river or small impounding reservoir.

9. A DISADVANTAGE of drawing a water supply from a large lake is that   9.____

    A. expensive treatment is required
    B. a limited quantity of water is available
    C. nearby cities may dump sewage into the lake
    D. the water is too cold

10. An ADVANTAGE of drawing a water supply from a large lake is that the   10.____

    A. water is uniform in quality
    B. water varies in temperature
    C. intake is distant from the shore
    D. intake may be near a sewer outlet

Questions 11-13.

DIRECTIONS: Questions 11 through 13 are to be answered SOLELY on the basis of the following paragraph.

Excavation of trench—The trench shall be excavated as directed; one side of the street or avenue shall be left open for traffic at all times. In paved streets, the length of trench that may be opened between the point where the backfilling has been completed and the point where the pavement is being removed shall not exceed fifteen hundred feet for pipes 24 inches or less in diameter. For pipes larger than 24-inch, the length of open trenches shall not exceed one thousand feet. The completion of the backfilling shall be interpreted to mean the backfilling of the trench and the consolidation of the backfill so that vehicular traffic can be resumed over the backfill, and also the placing of any temporary pavement that may be required.

11. According to the above paragraph, the street

    A. can be closed to traffic in emergencies
    B. can be closed to traffic only when laying more than 1500 feet of pipe
    C. is closed to traffic as directed
    D. shall be left open for traffic at all times

11._____

12. According to the above paragraph, the MAXIMUM length of open trench permitted in paved streets depends on the

    A. traffic on the street
    B. type of ground that is being excavated
    C. water conditions met with in excavation
    D. diameter of the pipe being laid

12._____

13. According to the above paragraph, the one of the following items that is included in the *completion of the backfilling* is

    A. sheeting and bracing   B. cradle
    C. temporary pavement   D. bridging

13._____

Questions 14-16.

DIRECTIONS: Questions 14 through 16 are to be answered SOLELY on the basis of the following paragraph.

The Contractor shall notify the Engineer by noon of the day immediately preceding the date when he wishes to shut down any main; and if the time set be approved, the Contractor shall provide the men necessary to shut down the main at the time stipulated, and to previously notify all consumers whose supply may be affected. These men shall be under the direction of the Department employees, who will superintend all operations of valves and hydrants. Shutdowns for making connections will not be made unless and until the Contractor has everything on the ground in readiness for the work.

14. According to the above paragraph, before a contractor can make a shut-down, he MUST notify the

    A. police department   B. District Foreman
    C. Engineer   D. Highway Department

14._____

15. According to the above paragraph, the operation of the valves will be supervised by the   15.____

    A. Department employees
    B. Contractor's men
    C. Contractor's superintendent
    D. Engineer

16. According to the above paragraph, shut-downs for connections are made   16.____

    A. the day before the connection is to be made
    B. first and then consumers are notified
    C. at any time convenient to the Contractor
    D. when the Contractor has everything on the ground in readiness for the work

Questions 17-22.

DIRECTIONS: Questions 17 through 22 are to be answered SOLELY on the basis of the following paragraphs.

HOT WATER GENERATION

The hot water that comes from a faucet is called Domestic Hot Water. It is heated by a steam coil that runs through a storage tank full of water in the basement of each building.

As the tenants take the hot water, fresh cold water enters the tank and is heated. The temperature of this water is automatically kept at approximately 140° F.

The device which controls the temperature is called a temperature regulator valve. It is operated by a bellows, capillary tube, and thermo bulb which connects between the valve and the hot water being stored in the tank. This bulb, tube, and bellows contains a liquid which expands and contracts with changes in temperatures.

As the water in the tank reaches 140° F, the liquid in the thermo bulb expands and causes pressure to travel along the capillary tube and into the bellows. The expanded liquid forces the bellows to push the Temperature Regulator Valve Stem down, closing the valve. No more steam can enter the coil in the tank, and the water will get no hotter.

As the hot water is used by the tenants, cold water enters the tank and pulls the temperature down. This causes the liquid in the thermo bulb to cool and contract (shrink). The pressure is no longer in the bellows, and a spring pushes it up, allowing the valve to open and allowing steam to again enter the heating coil in the storage tank, raising the temperature of the Domestic Hot Water to 140° F.

17. Domestic hot water is heated by   17.____

    A. coal   B. electricity
    C. hot water   D. steam

18. The temperature of domestic hot water is MOST NEARLY   18.____

    A. 75° F   B. 100° F   C. 140° F   D. 212° F

19. The temperature of the hot water is controlled by a   19._____

    A. thermometer
    B. temperature regulator valve
    C. pressuretrol
    D. pressure gauge

20. The temperature regulator valve is operated by a combination of a   20._____

    A. thermometer and a thermo bulb
    B. thermometer and a pyrometer
    C. bellows, capillary tube, and a thermometer
    D. bellows, capillary tube, and a thermo bulb

21. Closing of the temperature regulator valve prevents _____ from entering the heating   21._____
    coil in the tank.

    A. water   B. steam
    C. electricity   D. air

22. As hot water is used by the tenants, the temperature of the water in the tank   22._____

    A. increases   B. decreases
    C. remains the same   D. approaches 212° F

Question 23.

DIRECTIONS: Question 23 is to be answered SOLELY on the basis of the following para-
               graph.

Lack of service meters has a definite effect on water consumption. Metering of all services of a city should reduce consumption to about 50 percent of the consumption without
meters. Although metering reduces water consumption, there is a tendency for consumption to
increase gradually after all services are metered.

23. According to the above paragraph, the one of the following statements that is CORRECT   23._____
    is:

    A. Consumption of water is cut approximately in half by metering, but once all ser-
       vices are metered, the consumption then increases gradually
    B. After all services are metered, water consumption continues to decrease steadily
    C. Metering of all services reduces the consumption of water by much more than half
    D. Water consumption is not affected by metering of all services

Question 24.

DIRECTIONS: Questions 24 is to be answered SOLELY on the basis of the following para-
               graph.

A venturi meter operates without moving parts and hence is the simplest type of meter in
use so far as its construction is concerned. It is a velocity meter, and it is suitable for measuring
only high rates of flow. Rates of flow below its capacity limit are not accurately measured. It is,
therefore, not suitable for use in measuring the low intermittent demand of most consumers.

24. According to the above paragraph, the flow in a pipe which would MOST accurately be measured by a venturi meter is   24.____

    A. an intermittent flow below the meter's capacity
    B. a steady flow below the meter's capacity
    C. a steady flow at the meter's capacity
    D. intermittent flows above or below capacity of the meter

Question 25.

DIRECTIONS: Question 25 is to be answered SOLELY on the basis of the following paragraph.

    A house service water supply connection may be taken from the sprinkler water supply connection to the public main if the diameter of the house service water supply connection is not greater than onehalf the diameter of the sprinkler water supply connection. No shutoff valve shall be placed on the sprinkler supply line other than the main shut-off valve for the building on the street side of the house service water supply connection. If such a connection is made and if a tap also exists for the house service water supply, the tap shall be plugged.

25. According to the above paragraph, the one of the following statements that is CORRECT   25.____
    is:

    A. A sprinkler water supply connection should be at least twice the diameter of any house service water supply connection taken from it
    B. A shut-off valve, in addition to the main shut-off valve, is required on sprinkler supply lines on the street side of the house service water supply connection
    C. Where a house service water supply is connected to the sprinkler water supply and there is a tap for the house service water supply, the tap may remain in service
    D. A house service water supply connection may be taken off each side of the main shut-off valve of the sprinkler water supply

----

KEY (CORRECT ANSWERS)

1.	C		11.	D
2.	D		12.	D
3.	A		13.	C
4.	D		14.	C
5.	C		15.	A
6.	A		16.	D
7.	B		17.	D
8.	C		18.	C
9.	C		19.	B
10.	A		20.	D

21.	B
22.	B
23.	A
24.	C
25.	A

TEST 3

DIRECTIONS: Each question or incomplete statement is followed by several suggested answers or completions. Select the one that BEST answers the question or completes the statement. *PRINT THE LETTER OF THE CORRECT ANSWER IN THE SPACE AT THE RIGHT.*

Questions 1-4.

DIRECTIONS: Questions 1 through 4 are to be answered SOLELY on the basis of the following paragraph.

Welds in sheet metal up to 1/16 inch in thickness can be made satisfactorily by flanging the edges of the joint. The edges are prepared by turning up a very thin lip or flange along the line of the joint. The height of this flange should be equal to the thickness of the sheet being welded. The edges should be aligned so that the flanges stand up, and the joint should be tack-welded every 5 or 6 inches. Heavy angles or bars should be clamped on each side of the joint to prevent distortion or buckling. No filler metal is required for making this joint. The raised edges are quickly melted by the heat of the welding flame so as to produce an even weld bead which is nearly flush with the original sheet metal surface. By controlling the speed of welding and the motion of the flame, good fusion to the under side of the sheets can be obtained without burning through.

1. According to the above paragraph, satisfactory welds may be made in sheet metal by flanging the edges.
   The MAXIMUM thickness of metal recommended is

   A. 20 gauge   B. 18 gauge
   C. 1/16"   D. 5/64"

                                                                                1._____

2. According to the above paragraph, good fusion may be obtained without burning through of the metal by controlling the motion of the flame and the

   A. size of tip   B. speed of welding
   C. oxygen flow   D. acetylene flow

                                                                                2._____

3. According to the above paragraph, if the thickness of the metal is 1/32", then the flange height should be

   A. 1/64"   B. 1/32"   C. 1/16"   D. 1/8"

                                                                                3._____

4. According to the above paragraph, distortion in the welding of sheet metal may be prevented by

   A. controlling the speed of welding
   B. use of a flange of correct height
   C. use of proper filler metal
   D. clamping angles on each side of the joint

                                                                           4._____

Questions 5-12.

DIRECTIONS: Questions 5 through 12 are to be answered SOLELY on the basis of the Edison storage battery maintenance procedure below.

EDISON STORAGE BATTERY MAINTENANCE PROCEDURE

Take a voltage reading of each cell in the battery with a voltmeter. Any battery with two or more dead or reverse cells is to be removed and sent to the shop. All cell caps are to be opened, and the water level brought up to 2 3/4" above the plates. Any battery requiring a considerable amount of water must be called to the foreman's attention. All cell caps must be brushed clean and Edison battery oil applied to them. No batteries are to remain in service with cell caps broken or missing. The normal specific gravity reading of the solution must not be above 1.230 nor below 1.160. This reading is to be taken only on batteries which are found to be weak. Batteries with specific gravity lower than 1.160 must be sent to the shop. Be careful when disconnecting leads from the battery since a slight, turn of the connecting post will result in a dead cell due to the cell plates becoming short-circuited. When disconnecting leads, use a standard Edison terminal puller. When recording defective cells, give the battery number, the car number, and the position of the cell in the battery. No. 1 cell is the cell to which the positive battery lead is connected and so on up to the last cell, No. 26, to which the negative lead is connected.

5.   A normal specific gravity reading would be   5._____

    A. 1.450   B. 1.294   C. 1.200   D. 1.180

6.   Batteries with below normal specific gravity reading MUST   6._____

    A. always have water added
    B. be called to the foreman's attention
    C. not be given a voltmeter test
    D. be sent to the shop

7.   The battery leads are disconnected by using   7._____

    A. gas pliers
    B. Edison battery oil to free them
    C. a screwdriver to pry them off
    D. a standard Edison terminal puller

8.   To completely record a defective cell, _____ required.   8._____

    A. only one identifying number is
    B. two identifying numbers are
    C. three identifying numbers are
    D. four identifying numbers are

9.   A battery MUST be taken out of service if it has   9._____

    A. one dead cell   B. broken cell caps
    C. one reversed cell   D. a low water level

10.   The battery water level should be brought up above the plates by _____ inches.   10._____

    A. 2.75   B. 1.370   C. 1.264   D. 0.600

11. Specific gravity readings are to be taken only on batteries which 11.___

    A. are removed from service
    B. have missing cell caps
    C. are weak
    D. have a high water level

12. Dead cells are sometimes caused by 12.___

    A. a slight turn of the connecting post
    B. taking unnecessary gravity readings
    C. adding too little battery oil
    D. adding too much water

Questions 13-14.

DIRECTIONS: Questions 13 and 14 are to be answered SOLELY on the basis of the following paragraph.

It cannot be stressed too strongly that the greatest care should be taken in handling tools. If they are handled carelessly, serious accidents may result. Many accidents can be avoided if the back of the trowel is kept clean and if the trowel is not allowed to contain too much mortar. Where there is an *excess* of mortar, some might drop or splash into the plasterer's eyes. Any mortar which is dropped onto the hands, wrists, ankles, or underclothing should be removed immediately.

13. The MAIN point of the above paragraph is that 13.___

    A. all accidents will be avoided if tools are kept clean
    B. most accidents can be avoided by the use of protective gloves
    C. many accidents are caused by careless handling of tools
    D. trowels should be kept free of mortar at all times

14. In the above paragraph, the word *excess* means MOST NEARLY 14.___

    A. surplus   B. minor   C. scant   D. short

Questions 15-18.

DIRECTIONS: Questions 15 through 18 are to be answered SOLELY on the basis of the following paragraph.

There are two unfounded ideas that must be discarded before tackling the lube-simplification job. *Oil is oil* was a common expression from the middle of the nineteenth century up to the early 1900s. Then, as the century got well underway, *the pendulum swung in a wide arc.* At present, we find many oils being used, each with supposedly special properties. The large number of lube oils used at present results from the rapid growth at the same time of machine development and oil refining. The refiner acts to market new oils for each machine developed, and the machine manufacturer feels that each new mechanical unit is different from the others and needs a special lube oil. These feelings may be well-founded, but in many cases they are based on misinformation or blind faith in certain lube oil qualities. At the present time, operators and even lube engineers are finding it tough to keep track of all the claimed properties of all the lube oils.

15. It follows from the sense of this paragraph that the idea that *oil is oil* is unfounded because

    A. it was conceived in the middle of the nineteenth century
    B. the basic and varying properties of lube oils have now been shown to exist
    C. lube oil properties, though fully known, were kept secret for economic reasons
    D. there was no need for but one basic lube oil in the latter part of the nineteenth century

15.____

16. In the above paragraph, the phrase *the pendulum swung in a wide arc* means MOST NEARLY

    A. oil refining was unable to keep up with machinery development
    B. before 1900, lube oil engineers found it difficult to keep track of lube oil characteristics
    C. the simplification of lube oils and their application was developed about 1900
    D. many different lube oils with varying characteristics were marketed

16.____

17. As indicated in this paragraph, the simplification of the characteristics and the uses of lube oils is needed because the

    A. manufacturers develop new machines to overcome competition
    B. change in process at the refineries for a new lube oil is costly
    C. present market is flooded with many so-called *special purpose* lube oils
    D. *blind faith* of the operators in lube oil qualities should be rewarded

17.____

18. A reason given for the claimed need for special lube oil, as indicated in this paragraph, is that

    A. development of new lube oils created the need for new machine units
    B. lube oil engineers developed new tests and standards
    C. basic crudes, from which lube oil is obtained, allow different refining methods
    D. newly developed machines are so very different from each other

18.____

Questions 19-22.

DIRECTIONS: Questions 19 through 22 are to be answered SOLELY on the basis of the following paragraph.

ACCIDENT PREVENTION

Many accidents and injuries can be prevented if employees learn to be more careful. The wearing of shoes with thin or badly worn soles or open toes can easily lead to foot injuries from tacks, nails, and chair and desk legs. Loose or torn clothing should not be worn near moving machinery. This is especially true of neckties, which can very easily become caught in the machine. You should not place objects so that they block or partly block hallways, corridors, or other passageways. Even when they are stored in the proper place, tools, supplies, and equipment should be carefully placed or piled so as not to fall, nor have anything stick out from a pile. Before cabinets, lockers, or ladders are moved, the tops should be cleared of anything which might injure someone or fall off. If necessary, use a dolly to move these or other bulky objects.

Despite all efforts to avoid accidents and injuries, however, some will happen. If an employee is injured, no matter how small the injury, he should report it to his supervisor and have the injury treated. A small cut that is not attended to can easily become infected and can cause more trouble than some injuries which at first seem more serious. It never pays to take chances.

19. According to the above passage, the one statement that is NOT true is that   19._____

    A. by being more careful, employees can reduce the number of accidents that happen
    B. women should wear shoes with open toes for comfort when working
    C. supplies should be piled so that nothing is sticking out from the pile
    D. if an employee sprains his wrist at work, he should tell his supervisor about it

20. According to the above passage, you should NOT wear loose clothing when you are   20._____

    A. in a corridor
    B. storing tools
    C. opening cabinets
    D. near moving machinery

21. According to the above passage, before moving a ladder, you should   21._____

    A. test all rungs
    B. get a dolly to carry the ladder at all times
    C. remove everything from the top of the ladder which might fall off
    D. remove your necktie

22. According to the above passage, an employee who gets a slight cut should   22._____

    A. have it treated to help prevent infection
    B. know that a slight cut becomes more easily infected than a big cut
    C. pay no attention to it as it can't become serious
    D. realize that it is more serious than any other type of injury

Questions 23-25.

DIRECTIONS: Questions 23 through 25 are to be answered SOLELY on the basis of the following paragraph.

Keeping the city operating day and night requires the services of more than 400,000 civil service workers – roughly the number of people who live in Syracuse. This huge army of specialists works at more than 2,000 different jobs. The city's civil service workers are able to do everything that needs doing to keep our city running. Their only purpose is the well-being, comfort, and safety of the citizens of the city.

23. Of the following titles, the one that MOST nearly gives the meaning of the above paragraph is   23._____

    A. CIVIL SERVICE IN SYRACUSE
    B. EVERYONE WORKS
    C. JOB VARIETY
    D. SERVING THE CITY

24. According to the above paragraph, in order to keep the city operating 24 hours a day,   24.____

    A. half of the civil service workers work days and half work nights
    B. more than 400,000 civil service workers are needed on the day shift
    C. the city needs about as many civil service workers as there are people in Syracuse
    D. the services of some people who live in Syracuse is required

25. According to the above paragraph, it is MOST reasonable to assume that in the city's civil   25.____
service,

    A. a worker can do any job that needs doing
    B. each worker works at a different job
    C. some workers work at more than one job
    D. some workers work at the same jobs

KEY (CORRECT ANSWERS)

1.	C		11.	C
2.	B		12.	A
3.	B		13.	C
4.	D		14.	A
5.	C		15.	B
6.	D		16.	D
7.	D		17.	C
8.	C		18.	D
9.	B		19.	B
10.	A		20.	D

21. C
22. A
23. D
24. C
25. D

ARITHMETICAL REASONING
EXAMINATION SECTION
TEST 1

DIRECTIONS: Each question or incomplete statement is followed by several suggested answers or completions. Select the one that BEST answers the question or completes the statement. *PRINT THE LETTER OF THE CORRECT ANSWER IN THE SPACE AT THE RIGHT.*

1. _____

1.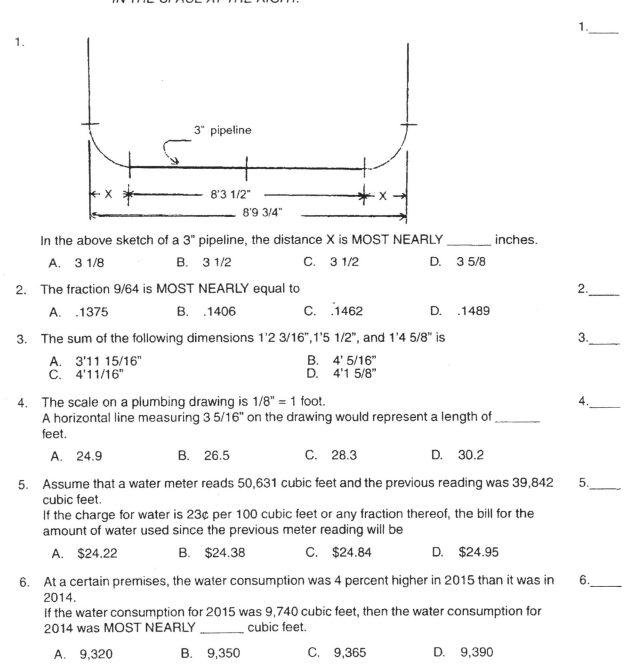

In the above sketch of a 3" pipeline, the distance X is MOST NEARLY _____ inches.

   A. 3 1/8   B. 3 1/2   C. 3 1/2   D. 3 5/8

2. The fraction 9/64 is MOST NEARLY equal to   2. _____

   A. .1375   B. .1406   C. .1462   D. .1489

3. The sum of the following dimensions 1'2 3/16",1'5 1/2", and 1'4 5/8" is   3. _____

   A. 3'11 15/16"   B. 4' 5/16"
   C. 4'11/16"   D. 4'1 5/8"

4. The scale on a plumbing drawing is 1/8" = 1 foot.   4. _____
   A horizontal line measuring 3 5/16" on the drawing would represent a length of _____ feet.

   A. 24.9   B. 26.5   C. 28.3   D. 30.2

5. Assume that a water meter reads 50,631 cubic feet and the previous reading was 39,842   5. _____
   cubic feet.
   If the charge for water is 23¢ per 100 cubic feet or any fraction thereof, the bill for the amount of water used since the previous meter reading will be

   A. $24.22   B. $24.38   C. $24.84   D. $24.95

6. At a certain premises, the water consumption was 4 percent higher in 2015 than it was in   6. _____
   2014.
   If the water consumption for 2015 was 9,740 cubic feet, then the water consumption for 2014 was MOST NEARLY _____ cubic feet.

   A. 9,320   B. 9,350   C. 9,365   D. 9,390

7. A pump delivers water at a constant rate of 40 gallons per minute.　　　　　　　　　7.____
   If there are 7.5 gallons to a cubic foot of water, the time it will take to fill a tank 6 feet x
   5 feet x 4 feet is MOST NEARLY _____ minutes.

   A. 15　　　　　　B. 22.5　　　　　　C. 28.5　　　　　　D. 30

8. The total weight, in pounds, of three lengths of 3" cast-iron pipe 7'6" long, weighing 14.5　8.____
   pounds per foot, and four lengths of 4" cast-iron pipe each 5'0" long, weighing 13.0
   pounds per foot, is MOST NEARLY

   A. 540　　　　　　B. 585　　　　　　C. 600　　　　　　D. 665

9. The water pressure at the bottom of a column of water 34 feet high is 14.7 lbs./sq.in.　　9.____
   The water pressure in lbs./sq.in. at the bottom of the column of water 12 feet high is
   MOST NEARLY

   A. 3　　　　　　B. 5　　　　　　C. 7　　　　　　D. 9

10. The number of cubic yards of earth that would be removed when digging a trench 8 feet　10.____
    wide x 9 feet deep x 63 feet long is

    A. 56　　　　　　B. 168　　　　　　C. 314　　　　　　D. 504

11. On test, a meter registered one cubic foot for each 1 1/3 cubic feet of water that passed　11.____
    through it.
    If the meter had a reading of 1,200 cubic feet, we may conclude that the CORRECT
    amount should be _____ cubic feet.

    A. 800　　　　　　B. 900　　　　　　C. 1,500　　　　　　D. 1,600

12. A water use meter reads 87,463 cubic feet.　　　　　　　　　　　　　　　　　　12.____
    If the previous reading was 17,377 cubic feet and the rate charged is 15 cents per 100
    cubic feet, the bill for water use during this period is about

    A. $45.00　　　　　B. $65.00　　　　　C. $85.00　　　　　D. $105.00

13. Under proper conditions, the one of the following groups of pipes that gives the same　13.____
    flow in gals/min as one 6" diameter pipe is (neglect friction) _____ pipes of _____
    diameter each.

    A. 3; 3"　　　　　B. 4; 3"　　　　　C. 2; 4"　　　　　D. 3; 4"

14. A roof tank is used to furnish the domestic water supply to a ten story building. This tank　14.____
    has a capacity of 5,900 gallons. At 10:00 A.M. one morning, the tank is half full.
    If water is being used at the rate of 50 gals/min, the pump which is used to fill the tank
    has a rated capacity of 90 gals/min, the time it would take to fill the tank
    under these conditions is MOST NEARLY _____ hour(s),
    _____ minutes.

    A. 2; 8　　　　　B. 1; 14　　　　　C. 2; 32　　　　　D. 1; 2

15. The number of gallons of water contained in a cylindrical swimming pool 8 feet in diame-　15.____
    ter and filled to a depth of 3 feet 6 inches is MOST NEARLY (assume 7.5 gallons = 1
    cubic foot)

    A. 30　　　　　　B. 225　　　　　　C. 1,320　　　　　　D. 3,000

16. The charge for metered water is 52 1/2 cents per hundred cubic feet, with a minimum charge of $21 per annum. Of the following, the SMALLEST water usage in hundred cubic feet that would result in a charge GREATER than the minimum is

    A. 39   B. 40   C. 41   D. 42

16.____

17. The annual frontage rent on a one-story building 40 ft. in length is $735.00. For each additional story, $52.50 per annum is added to the frontage rent. For demolition, the charge for wetting down is 3/8 of the annual frontage charge.
    The charge for wetting down a building six stories in height, with a 40 ft. frontage, is MOST NEARLY

    A. $369   B. $371   C. $372   D. $374

17.____

18. If the drawing of a piping layout is made to a scale of 1/4" equals one foot, then a 7'9" length of piping would be represented by a scaled length on the drawing of APPROXI-MATELY _____ inches.

    A. 2   B. 7 3/4   C. 23 1/4   D. 31

18.____

19. A plumbing sketch is drawn to a scale of eighth-size. A line measuring 3" on the sketch would be equivalent to _____ feet.

    A. 2   B. 6   C. 12   D. 24

19.____

20. If 500 feet of pipe weighs 800 lbs., the number of pounds that 120 feet will weigh is MOST NEARLY

    A. 190   B. 210   C. 230   D. 240

20.____

21. If a trench is excavated 3'0" wide by 5'6" deep and 50 feet long, the total number of cubic yards of earth removed is MOST NEARLY

    A. 30   B. 90   C. 150   D. 825

21.____

22. Assume that a plumber earns $86,500 per year.
    If eighteen percent of his pay is deducted for taxes and social security, his net weekly pay will be APPROXIMATELY

    A. $1,326   B. $1,365   C. $1,436   D. $1,457.50

22.____

23. Assume that a plumbing installation is made up of the following fixtures and groups of fix-tures: 12 bathroom groups each containing one W.C., one lavatory, and one bathtub with shower; 12 bathroom groups each containing one W.C., one lavatory, one bathtub, and one shower stall; 24 combination kitchen fixtures; 4 floor drains; 6 slop sinks without flushing rim; and 2 shower stalls (or shower bath).
    The total number of fixtures for the above plumbing installation is MOST NEARLY

    A. 60   B. 95   C. 120   D. 210

23.____

24. A triangular opening in a wall forms a 30-60 degree right triangle.
    If the longest side measures 12'0", then the shortest side will measure

    A. 3'0"   B. 4'0"   C. 6'0"   D. 8'0"

24.____

25. You are directed to cut 4 pieces of pipe, one each of the following length: 2'6 1/4",   25.____
3'9 3/8", 4'7 5/8", and 5'8 7/8".
The total length of these 4 pieces is

    A. 15'7 1/4"   B. 15'9 3/8"   C. 16'5 7/8"   D. 16'8 1/8"

KEY (CORRECT ANSWERS)

1.	A		11.	D
2.	B		12.	D
3.	B		13.	B
4.	B		14.	B
5.	C		15.	C
6.	C		16.	C
7.	B		17.	D
8.	B		18.	A
9.	B		19.	A
10.	B		20.	A

21.	A
22.	B
23.	C
24.	C
25.	D

---

5 (#1)

SOLUTIONS TO PROBLEMS

1. 8'3 1/2" + x + x = 8'9 3/4" Then, 2x = 6 1/4", so x = 3 1/8"

2. 9/64 = .140625 = .1406

3. 1'2 3/16" + 1'5 1/2" +1'4 5/8" = 3'11 21/16" = 4'5/16"

4. 3 5/16" ÷ 1/8" =53/16 x 8/1 = 26.5. Then, (26.5)(1 ft.) = 26.5 feet

5. 50,631 - 39,842 = 10,789; 10,789 ÷ 100 = 107.89
    Since the cost is .23 per 100 cubic feet or any fraction thereof, the cost will be
    (.23)(107) + .23 = $24.84

6. 9740 ÷ 1.04 = 9365 cu.ft.

7. 40 ÷ 7.5 = 5 1/3 cu.ft. of water per minute. The volume = (6)(5)(4) = 120 cu.ft. Thus, the number of minutes needed to fill the tank is 120 ÷ 5 1/3 = 22.5

8. 3" pipe: 3 x 7'6" = 22 1/2' x 14.5 lbs. = 326.25
    4" pipe: 4 x 5' = 20' x 13 lbs. = 260
    326.25 + 260 = 586.25 (most nearly 585)

9. Let x = pressure. Then, 34/12 = 14.7/x. So, 34x = 176.4
    Solving, x $\approx$ 5 lbs./sq.in.

10. (8)(9)(63) = 4536 cu.ft. Since 1 cu.yd. = 27 cu.ft., 4536 cu.ft. is equivalent to 168 cu.yds.

11. Let x = correct amount. Then, $\dfrac{1}{1200} = \dfrac{1\frac{1}{3}}{x}$. Solving, x = 1600

12. 87,463 - 17,377 = 70,086; and 70,086 ÷ 100 = 700.86 $\approx$ 700 Then, (700)(.15) = $105.00

13. Cross-sectional area of a 6" diameter pipe = $(\pi)(3")^2 = 9\pi$ sq. in. Note that the combined cross-sectional areas of four 3" diameter pipes = $(4)(\pi)(1.5")^2 = 9\pi$ sq. in.

14. 90 - 50 = 40 gals/min. Then, 2950 ÷ 40 = 73.75 min. $\approx$ 1 hr. 14 min.

15. Volume = $(\pi)(4)^2(3\ 1/2) = 56\pi$ cu.ft. Then, $(56\pi)(7.5) = 1320$ gals.

16. For 4100 cu.ft., the charge of (.525)(41) = $21,525 > $21

17. Rent = $73,500 + (5)($52.50) = $997,50. For demolition, the charge = (3/8)($997.50) $374

18. (1/4")(7.75) = 2"

19. (3")(8) = 24" = 2 ft.

20. Let x = weight. Then, 500/800 = 120/x . Solving, x = 192 190 lbs.

21. (3')(5 1/2')(50') = 825 cu.ft. Then, 825 ÷ 27 ≈ 30 cu.yds.

22. Net pay = (.82)($86,500) = $70,930/yr. Weekly pay = $70,930 ÷ 52 ≈ $1365

23. (12x3) + (12x4) +24+4+6+2= 120

24. The shortest side = (1/2)(hypotenuse) = (1/2)(12') = 6'

25. 2'6 1/4" + 3'9 3/8" + 4'7 5/8" + 5'8 7/8 " = 14'30 17/8" = 16'8 1/8"

TEST 2

DIRECTIONS: Each question or incomplete statement is followed by several suggested answers or completions. Select the one that BEST answers the question or completes the statement. *PRINT THE LETTER OF THE CORRECT ANSWER IN THE SPACE AT THE RIGHT.*

1. The sum of the following pipe lengths, 15 5/8", 8 3/4", 30 5/16" and 20 1/2", is

   A. 77 1/8"   B. 76 3/16"   C. 75 3/16"   D. 74 5/16"

1.____

2. If the outside diameter of a pipe is 6 inches and the wall thickness is 1/2 inch, the inside area of this pipe, in square inches, is MOST NEARLY

   A. 15.7   B. 17.3   C. 19.6   D. 23.8

2.____

3. Three lengths of pipe 1'10", 3'2 1/2", and 5'7 1/2", respectively, are to be cut from a pipe 14'0" long.
Allowing 1/8" for each pipe cut, the length of pipe remaining is

   A. 3'1 1/8"   B. 3'2 1/2"   C. 3'3 1/4"   D. 3'3 5/8"

3.____

4. According to the building code, the MAXIMUM permitted surface temperature of combustible construction materials located near heating equipment is 76.5°C. ($^{o}F=(^{o}Cx9/5)+32$)
Maximum temperature Fahrenheit is MOST NEARLY

   A. 170° F   B. 195° F   C. 210° F   D. 220° F

4.____

5. A pump discharges 7.5 gals/minutes.
In 2.5 hours the pump will discharge _____ gallons.

   A. 1125   B. 1875   C. 1950   D. 2200

5.____

6. A pipe with an outside diameter of 4" has a circumference of MOST NEARLY _____ inches.

   A. 8.05   B. 9.81   C. 12.57   D. 14.92

6.____

7. A piping sketch is drawn to a scale of 1/8" = 1 foot.
A vertical steam line measuring 3 1/2" on the sketch would have an ACTUAL length of _____ feet.

   A. 16   B. 22   C. 24   D. 28

7.____

8. A pipe having an inside diameter of 3.48 inches and a wall thickness of .18 inches will have an outside diameter of _____ inches.

   A. 3.84   B. 3.64   C. 3.57   D. 3.51

8.____

9. A rectangular steel bar having a volume of 30 cubic inches, a width of 2 inches, and a height of 3 inches will have a length of _____ inches.

   A. 12   B. 10   C. 8   D. 5

9.____

10. A pipe weighs 20.4 pounds per foot of length.
The total weight of eight pieces of this pipe with each piece 20 feet in length is MOST NEARLY _____ pounds.

   A. 460   B. 1,680   C. 2,420   D. 3,260

10.____

11. Assume that four pieces of pipe measuring 2'1 1/4", 4'2 3/4", 5'1 9/16", and 6'3 5/8",   11.____
    respectively, are cut with a saw from a pipe 20"0' long.
    Allowing 1/16" waste for each cut, the length of the remaining pipe is

    A. 2'1 9/16"   B. 2'2 9/16"   C. 2'4 13/16"   D. 2'8 9/16"

12. If one cubic inch of steel weighs 0.28 pounds, the weight, in pounds, of a steel bar 1/2" x   12.____
    6" x 2'0" long is MOST NEARLY

    A. 11   B. 16   C. 20   D. 24

13. If the circumference of a circle is equal to 31.416 inches, then its diameter, in inches, is   13.____
    equal to MOST NEARLY

    A. 8   B. 9   C. 10   D. 13

14. Assume that a steam fitter's helper receives a salary of $171.36 a day for 250 days is   14.____
    considered a full work year. If taxes, social security, hospitalization, and pension
    deducted from his salary amounts to 16 percent of his gross pay, then his net yearly sal-
    ary will be MOST NEARLY

    A. $31,788   B. $35,982   C. $41,982   D. $42,840

15. If the outside diameter of a pipe is 14 inches and the wall thickness is 1/2 inch, then the   15.____
    inside area of the pipe, in square inches, is MOST NEARLY

    A. 125   B. 133   C. 143   D. 154

16. A steam leak in a pipe line allows steam to escape at a rate of 50,000 pounds each   16.____
    month.
    Assuming that the cost of steam is $2.50 per 1,000 pounds, the TOTAL cost of wasted
    steam from this leak for a 12-month period would amount to

    A. $125   B. $300   C. $1,500   D. $3,000

17. If 250 feet of 4" pipe weighs 400 pounds, the weight of this pipe per linear foot is _____   17.____
    pounds.

    A. 1.25   B. 1.50   C. 1.60   D. 1.75

18. A set of heating plan drawings is drawn to a scale of 1/4" = 1 foot.   18.____
    If a length of pipe measures 4 5/8" on the drawing, the ACTUAL length of the pipe, in
    feet, is

    A. 16.3   B. 16.8   C. 17.5   D. 18.5

19. The TOTAL length of four pieces of pipe whose lengths are 3'4 1/2", 2'1 5/16", 4'9 3/8",   19.____
    and 2'3 1/4", respectively, is

    A. 11'5 7/16"   B. 11'6 7/16"
    C. 12'5 7/16"   D. 12'6 7/16"

20. Assume that a pipe trench is 3 feet wide, 3 feet deep, and 300 feet long.   20.____
    If the unit cost of excavating the trench is $120 per cubic yard, the TOTAL cost of exca-
    vating the trench is

    A. $1,200   B. $12,000   C. $27,000   D. $36,000

21. The TOTAL length of four pieces of 1 1/2" galvanized steel pipe whose lengths are 7 ft. + 3 1/2 inches, 4 ft. + 2 1/4 inches, 6 ft. + 7 inches, and 8 ft. +5 1/8 inches is   21.____

    A. 26 feet + 5 7/8 inches   B. 25 ft. + 6 7/8 inches
    C. 25 feet + 4 1/4 inches   D. 25 ft. + 3 3/8 inches

22. A swimming pool is 25' wide by 75' long and has an average depth of 5'. 1 cubic foot contains 7.5 gallons of water. The capacity, when filled to the overflow, is _____ gallons.   22.____

    A. 9,375   B. 65,625   C. 69,005   D. 70,312

23. The sum of 3 1/4, 5 1/8, 2 1/2 , and 3 3/8 is   23.____

    A. 14   B. 14 1/8   C. 14 1/4   D. 14 3/8

24. Assume that it takes 6 men 8 days to do a particular job. If you have only 4 men available to do this job and they all work at the same speed, then the number of days it would take to complete the job would be   24.____

    A. 11   B. 12   C. 13   D. 14

25. The total length of four pieces of 2" O.D. pipe, whose lengths are 7'3 1/2", 4'2 3/16", 5'7 5/16", and 8'5 7/8", respectively, is MOST NEARLY   25.____

    A. 24'6 3/4"   B. 24'7 15/16"
    C. 25'5 13/16"   D. 25'6 7/8"

KEY (CORRECT ANSWERS)

1. C		11. B
2. C		12. C
3. D		13. C
4. A		14. B
5. A		15. B
6. C		16. C
7. D		17. C
8. A		18. D
9. D		19. D
10. D		20. B

21.	A
22.	D
23.	C
24.	B
25.	D

SOLUTIONS TO PROBLEMS

1. 15 5/8" + 8 3/4" + 30 5/16" + 20 1/2" = 73 35/16" = 75 3/16"

2. Inside diameter = 6" - 1/2" - 1/2" = 5". Area = $(\pi)(5/2")^2 \approx 19.6$ sq. in.

3. Pipe remaining = 14' - 1'10" - 3'2 1/2" - 5'7 1/2" - (3)(1/8") = 3'3 5/8"

4. 76.5 x 9/5 = 137.7 + 32 = 169.7

5. 7.5 x 150 = 1125

6. Radius = 2" Circumference = $(2\pi)(2") \approx 12.57"$

7. 3 1/2" 1/8" = (7/2)(8/1) = 28 Then, (28)(1 ft.) = 28 feet

8. Outside diameter = 3.48" + .18" + .18" = 3.84"

9. 30 = (2)(3)(length). So, length = 5"

10. Total weight = (20.4)(8)(20) $\approx$ 3260 lbs.

11. 20' - 2'1 1/4" - 4'2 3/4" - 5'1 9/16" - 6'3 5/8" - (4)(1/16") = 2'2 9/16"

12. Weight = (.28)(1/2")(6")(24") = 20.16 $\approx$ 20 lbs.

13. Diameter = 31.416" $\div \pi \approx$ 10"

14. His net pay for 250 days = (.84)($171.36)(250) = $35,985.60 $\approx$ $35,928 (from answer key)

15. Inside diameter = 14" - 1/2" - 1/2" = 13". Area = $(\pi)(13/2")^2 \approx$ 133 sq.in

16. (50,000 lbs.)(12) = 600,000 lbs. per year. The cost would be ($2.50)(600) = $1500

17. 400 $\div$ 250 = 1.60 pounds per linear foot

18. 4 5/8" $\div$ 1/4" = 37/8 . 4/1 = 18.5 Then, (18.5)(1 ft.) = 18.5 feet

19. 3'4 1/2" + 2'1 5/16" + 4'9 3/8" + 2'3 1/4" = 11'17 23/16" = 12'6 7/16"

20. (3')(3')(300') = 2700 cu.ft., which is 2700 $\div$ 27 = 100 cu.yds. Total cost = ($120)(100) = $12,000

21. 7'3 1/2" + 4'2 1/4" + 6'7" + 8'5 1/8" = 25'17 7/8" = 26'5 7/8"

22. (25)(75)(5) = 9375 cu.ft. Then, (9375)(7.5) $\approx$ 70,312 gals.

23. 3 1/4 + 5 1/8 + 2 1/2 + 3 3/8 = 13 10/8 = 14 1/4

24. (6) (8) = 48 man-days. Then, 48 $\div$ 4 = 12 days

25. 7'3 1/2" + 4'2 3/16" + 5'7 5/16" + 8'5 7/8"= 24'17 30/16" = 25'6 7/8"

TEST 3

DIRECTIONS: Each question or incomplete statement is followed by several suggested answers or completions. Select the one that BEST answers the question or completes the statement. *PRINT THE LETTER OF THE CORRECT ANSWER IN THE SPACE AT THE RIGHT.*

1. The time required to pump 2,500 gallons of water out of a sump at the rate of 12 1/2 gallons per minutes would be _____ hour(s) _____ minutes.

     A.   1; 40   B.   2; 30   C.   3; 20   D.   6; 40

2. Copper tubing which has an inside diameter of 1 1/16" and a wall thickness of .095" has an outside diameter which is MOST NEARLY _____ inches.

     A.   1 5/32   B.   1 3/16   C.   1 7/32   D.   1 1/4

3. Assume that 90 gallons per minute flow through a certain 3-inch pipe which is tapped into a street main.
     The amount of water which would flow through a 1-inch pipe tapped into the same street main is MOST NEARLY _____ gpm.

     A.   90   B.   45   C.   30   D.   10

4. The weight of a 6 foot length of 8-inch pipe which weighs 24.70 pounds per foot is _____ lbs.

     A.   148.2   B.   176.8   C.   197.6   D.   212.4

5. If a 4-inch pipe is directly coupled to a 2-inch pipe and 16 gallons per minute are flowing through the 4-inch pipe, then the flow through the 2-inch pipe will be _____ gallons per minute.

     A.   4   B.   8   C.   16   D.   32

6. If the water pressure at the bottom of a column of water 34 feet high is 14.7 pounds per square inch, the water pressure at the bottom of a column of water 18 feet high is MOST NEARLY _____ pounds per square inch.

     A.   8.0   B.   7.8   C.   7.6   D.   7.4

7. If there are 7 1/2 gallons in a cubic foot of water and if water flows from a hose at a constant rate of 4 gallons per minute, the time it should take to COMPLETELY fill a tank of 1,600 cubic feet capacity with water from that hose is _____ hours.

     A.   300   B.   150   C.   100   D.   50

8. Each of a group of fifteen water meter readers read an average of 62 water meters a day in a certain 5-day work week. A total of 5,115 meters are read by this group the following week.
     The TOTAL number of meters read in the second week as compared to the first week shows a

     A.   10% increase   B.   15% increase
     C.   20% increase   D.   5% decrease

1._____
2._____
3._____
4._____
5._____
6._____
7._____
8._____

9. A certain water consumer used 5% more water in 1994 than he did in 1993.   9.____
   If his water consumption for 1994 was 8,375 cubic feet, the amount of water he consumed in 1993 was MOST NEARLY _____ cubic feet.

   A. 9,014   B. 8,816   C. 7,976   D. 6,776

10. Assume that a water meter reads 40,175 cubic feet and that the previous reading was   10.____
    29,186 cubic feet.
    If the charge for water is 92 cents per 100 cubic feet or any fraction thereof, the bill for
    the amount of water used since the previous meter reading should be

    A. $100.28   B. $101.04   C. $101.08   D. $101.20

11. A leaking faucet caused a loss of 216 cubic feet of water in a 30-day month.   11.____
    If there are 7.5 gallons in a cubic foot of water, then the AVERAGE loss of water per
    hour for that month was _____ gallons.

    A. 2 1/4   B. 2 1/8   C. 2   D. 1 3/4

12. The fraction which is equal to .375 is   12.____

    A. 3/16   B. 5/32   C. 3/8   D. 5/12

13. A square backyard swimming pool, each side of which is 10 feet long, is filled to a depth   13.____
    of 3 1/2 feet.
    If there are 7 1/2 gallons in a cubic foot of water, the number of gallons of water in the
    pool is MOST NEARLY _____ gallons.

    A. 46.7   B. 100   C. 2,625   D. 3,500

14. When 1 5/8, 3 3/4, 6 1/3, and 9 1/2 are added, the resulting sum is   14.____

    A. 21 1/8   B. 21 1/6   C. 21 5/24   D. 21 1/4

15. When 946 1/2 is subtracted from 1,035 1/4, the result is   15.____

    A. 87 1/4   B. 87 3/4   C. 88 1/4   D. 88 3/4

16. When 39 is multiplied by 697, the result is   16.____

    A. 8,364   B. 26,283   C. 27,183   D. 28,003

17. When 16.074 is divided by .045, the result is   17.____

    A. 3.6   B. 35.7   C. 357.2   D. 3,572

18. To dig a trench 3'0" wide, 50'0" long, and 5'6" deep, the total number of cubic yards of   18.____
    earth to be removed is MOST NEARLY

    A. 30   B. 90   C. 140   D. 825

19. The TOTAL length of four pieces of 2" pipe, whose lengths are 7'3 1/2", 4'2 3/16",   19.____
    5'7 5/16", and 8'5 7/8", respectively, is

    A. 24'6 3/4"   B. 24'7 15/16"
    C. 25'5 13/16"   D. 25'6 7/8"

20. A hot water line made of copper has a straight horizontal run of 150 feet and, when installed, is at a temperature of 45° F. In use, its temperature rises to 190° F. If the coefficient of expansion for copper is 0.0000095" per foot per degree F, the TOTAL expansion, in inches, in the run of pipe is given by the product of 150 multiplied by 0.0000095 by

   A. 145
   C. 145 divided by 12
   B. 145 x 12
   D. 145 x 12 x 12

21. A water storage tank measures 5' long, 4' wide, and 6' deep and is filled to the 5 1/2' mark with water.
If one cubic foot of water weighs 62 pounds, the number of pounds of water required to COMPLETELY fill the tank is

   A. 7,440   B. 6,200   C. 1,240   D. 620

22. Assume that a pipe worker earns $83,125.00 per year.
If seventeen percent of his pay is deducted for taxes, social security, and pension, his net weekly pay will be APPROXIMATELY

   A. $1598.50   B. $1504.00   C. $1453.00   D. $1325.00

23. If eighteen feet of 4" cast iron pipe weighs approximately 390 pounds, the weight of this pipe per lineal foot will be MOST NEARLY _____ lbs.

   A. 19   B. 22   C. 23   D. 25

24. If it takes 3 men 11 days to dig a trench, the number of days it will take 5 men to dig the same trench, assuming all work is done at the same rate of speed, is MOST NEARLY

   A. 6 1/2   B. 7 3/4   C. 8 1/4   D. 8 3/4

25. If a trench is dug 6'0" deep, 2'6" wide, and 8'0" long, the area of the opening, in square feet, is MOST NEARLY

   A. 48   B. 32   C. 20   D. 15

KEY (CORRECT ANSWERS)

1.	C	11.	A
2.	D	12.	C
3.	D	13.	C
4.	A	14.	C
5.	B	15.	D
6.	B	16.	C
7.	D	17.	C
8.	A	18.	A
9.	C	19.	D
10.	D	20.	A

21.	D
22.	D
23.	B
24.	A
25.	C

———

SOLUTIONS TO PROBLEMS

1. 2500 ÷ 12 1/2 = 200 min. = 3 hrs. 20 min.

2. 1 1/16" + .095" + .095" = 1.0625 + .095 + .095 = 1.2525" ≈ 1 1/4"

3. Cross-sectional areas for a 3-inch pipe and a 1-inch pipe are $(\pi)(1.5)^2$ and $(\pi)(.5)^2 =$ 2.25 π and .25 π, respectively. Let x = amount of water flowing through the 1-inch pipe. Then, $\dfrac{90}{x} = \dfrac{2.25\pi}{.25\pi}$. Solving, x = 10 gals/min

4. (24.70)(6) = 148.2 lbs.

5. $\dfrac{4" \text{ pipe}}{16 \text{ gallons}} = \dfrac{2" \text{ pipe}}{x \text{ gallons}}$, 4x = 32, x = 8

6. Let x = pressure. Then, 34/18 = 14.7/x . Solving, x ≈ 7.8

7. (1600)(7.5) = 12,000 gallons. Then, 12,000 ÷ 4 = 3000 min. = 50 hours

8. (15)(62)(5) = 4650. Then, (5115-4650)/4650 = 10% increase

9. 8375 ÷ 1.05 ≈ 7976 cu.ft.

10. 40,175 - 29,186 = 10,989 cu.ft. Then, 10,989 100 = 109.89. Since .92 is charged for each 100 cu.ft. or fraction thereof, total cost = (.92)(110) = $101.20

11. (216)(7.5) = 1620 gallons. In 30 days, there are 720 hours. Thus, the average water loss per hour = 1620 ÷ 720 = 2 1/4 gallons.

12. .375 = 375/1000 = 3/8

13. Volume = (10)(10)(3 1/2) = 350 cu.ft. Then, (350)(7 1/2) = 2625 gallons

14. 1 5/8 + 3 3/4 + 6 1/3 + 9 1/2 = 19 53/24 = 21 5/24

15. 1035 1/4 - 946 1/2 = 88 3/4

16. (39)(697) = 27,183

17. 16.074 .045 = 357.2

18. (3')(50')(5 1/2') = 825 cu.ft. ≈ 30 cu.yds., since 1 cu.yd. = 27 cu.ft.

19. 7'3 1/2" + 4'2 3/16" + 5'7 5/16" + 8'5 7/8" = 24'17 30/16" = 25'6 7/8"

20. Total expansion = (150)(.0000095)(145)

21. Number of pounds needed = (5) (4)(6-5 1/2)(62) = 620

22. Net annual pay = ($83,125)(.83) $\approx$ $69000. Then, the net weekly pay = $69000 ÷ 52 $\approx$ $1325 (actually about $1327)

23. 390 lbs. ÷ 18 = 21.6 lbs. per linear foot

24. (3)(11) = 33 man-days. Then, 33 ÷ 5 = 6.6 $\approx$ 6 1/2 days

25. Area = (8')(2 1/2') = 20 sq.ft.

—————

ARITHMETICAL REASONING

EXAMINATION SECTION
TEST 1

DIRECTIONS: Each question or incomplete statement is followed by several suggested answers or completions. Select the one that BEST answers the question or completes the statement. *PRINT THE LETTER OF THE CORRECT ANSWER IN THE SPACE AT THE RIGHT.*

1. If it takes 2 men 9 days to do a job, how many men are needed to do the same job in 3 days?

    A. 4   B. 5   C. 6   D. 7

1._____

2. Suppose that a department operates 1,644 buildings. If one employee is needed for every 2 buildings, and one foreman is needed for every 18 employees, the number of foremen needed is CLOSEST to

    A. 45   B. 50   C. 55   D. 60

2._____

3. If 60 bars of soap cost the same as 2 gallons of wax, how many bars of soap can be bought for the price of 5 gallons of wax?

    A. 120   B. 150   C. 180   D. 300

3._____

4. An employee waxes 275 sq.ft. of floor on Monday, 352 sq.ft. on Tuesday, 179 sq.ft. on Wednesday, and 302 sq.ft. on Thursday.
In order to average 280 sq.ft. of floor waxed a day, how many square feet of floor must he wax on Friday?

    A. 264   B. 278   C. 292   D. 358

4._____

5. A project covers 35 acres altogether. Lawns, playgrounds, and walks take up 28 acres and the rest is given over to buildings.
What percentage of the total area is given over to buildings?

    A. 7%   B. 20%   C. 25%   D. 28%

5._____

6. When preparing for a mopping operation, fill the standard 16 quart bucket to the 3/4 full mark with warm water. Then add detergent at the rate of 2 oz. per gallon of water and disinfectant at the rate of 1 oz. to 3 gallons of water. According to these directions, the amount of detergent and disinfectant to add to 3/4 of a bucket of warm water is _____ oz. detergent and _____ oz. disinfectant.

    A. 4; 1/2   B. 5; 3/4   C. 6; 1   D. 8; 1 1/4

6._____

7. If corn brooms weigh 32 lbs. a dozen, the average weight of one corn broom is CLOS-EST to _____ lbs. _____ oz.

    A. 2; 14   B. 2; 11   C. 2; 9   D. 2; 6

7._____

8. At the beginning of the year, a foreman has 7 dozen electric bulbs in stock. During the   8._____
   year, he receives a shipment of 14 dozen bulbs, and also replaces 5 burned out bulbs a
   month in each of 3 buildings in his area. How many electric bulbs does he have on
   hand at the end of the year? _____dozen.

   A. 3   B. 6   C. 8   D. 12

9. A project has 4 buildings, each 14 floors high. Each floor has 10 apartments.   9._____
   If 35% of the apartments in the project have 3 rooms or less, how many apartments
   have 4 or more rooms?

   A. 196   B. 210   C. 364   D. 406

10. An employee takes 1 hour and 30 minutes a day to sweep 30 flights of stairs.   10._____
    How many flights of stairs does he sweep in a month if he spends a total of 30 hours
    doing this job and works at the same rate?

    A. 200   B. 300   C. 600   D. 900

11. During a month, Employee A washed 30 windows, Employee B washed 4 times as many   11._____
    windows as Employee A, and Employee C washed half as many windows as Employee B.
    The TOTAL number of windows washed by all three men together during this month is

    A. 180   B. 210   C. 240   D. 330

12. How much would it cost to completely   12._____
    fence in the playground area shown at
    the right with fencing costing $7.50 a
    foot?
    A. $615.00
    B. $820.00
    C. $885.00
    D. $960.00

    14 FT.
    9 FT.
    26 FT.
    33 FT.

13. A drill bit measures .625 inches. The fractional equivalent, in inches, is   13._____

    A. 9/16   B. 5/8   C. 11/16   D. 3/4

14. The number of cubic yards of sand required to fill a bin measuring 12 feet by 6 feet by 4   14._____
    feet is MOST NEARLY

    A. 8   B. 11   C. 48   D. 96

15. Assume that you are assigned to put down floor tiles in a room measuring 8 feet by 10   15._____
    feet. Individual tiles measure 9 inches by 9 inches.
    The total number of floor tiles required to cover the entire floor is MOST NEARLY

    A. 107   B. 121   C. 142   D. 160

16. Lumber is usually sold by the board foot, and a board foot is defined as a board one foot square and one inch thick.
If the price of one board foot of lumber is 90 cents and you need 20 feet of lumber 6 inches wide and 1 inch thick, the cost of the 20 feet of lumber is

   A. $9.00   B. $12.00   C. $18.00   D. $24.00

16.____

17. For a certain plumbing repair job, you need three lengths of pipe, 12 1/4 inches, 6 1/2 inches, and 8 5/8 inches.
If you cut these three lengths from the same piece of pipe, which is 36 inches long, and each cut consumes 1/8 inch of pipe, the length of pipe REMAINING after you have cut out your three pieces should be _____ inches.

   A. 7 1/4   B. 7 7/8   C. 8 1/4   D. 8 7/8

17.____

18. A maintenance bond for a roadway pavement is in an amount of 10% of the estimated cost.
If the estimated cost is $8,000,000, the maintenance bond is

   A. $8,000   B. $80,000   C. $800,000   D. $8,000,000

18.____

19. Specifications require that a core be taken every 700 square yards of paved roadway or fraction thereof. A 100 foot by 200 foot rectangular area would require _____ core(s).

   A. 1   B. 2   C. 3   D. 4

19.____

20. An applicant must file a map at a scale of 1" = 40'. Six inches on the map represents _____ feet on the ground.

   A. 600   B. 240   C. 120   D. 60

20.____

21. A 100' x 110' lot has an area of MOST NEARLY _____ acre.

   A. 1/8   B. 1/4   C. 3/8   D. 1/2

21.____

22. 1 inch is MOST NEARLY equal to _____ feet.

   A. .02   B. .04   C. .06   D. .08

22.____

23. The area of the triangle EFG shown at the right is MOST NEARLY _____ sq. ft.

   A. 36   B. 42   C. 48   D. 54

23.____

24. Specifications state: As further security for the faithful performance of this contract, the Comptroller shall deduct, and retain until the final payment, 10% of the value of the work certified for payment in each partial payment voucher, until the amount so deducted and retained shall equal 5% of the contract price or in the case of a unit price contract, 5% of the estimated amount to be paid to the Contractor under the contract.
For a $300,000 contract, the amount to be retained at the end of the contract is

   A. $5,000   B. $10,000   C. $15,000   D. $20,000

24.____

25. Asphalt was laid for a length of 210 feet on the entire width of a street whose curb-to-curb distance is 30 feet. The number of square yards covered with asphalt is MOST NEARLY

   A. 210   B. 700   C. 2,100   D. 6,300

25.____

KEY (CORRECT ANSWERS)

1.	C		11.	B
2.	A		12.	C
3.	B		13.	B
4.	C		14.	B
5.	B		15.	C
6.	C		16.	A
7.	B		17.	C
8.	B		18.	C
9.	C		19.	D
10.	C		20.	B

21.	B
22.	D
23.	A
24.	C
25.	B

————————

SOLUTIONS TO PROBLEMS

1. (2)(9) = 18 man-days. Then, 18 ÷ 3 = 6 men

2. The number of employees = 1644 ÷ 2 = 822. The number of foremen needed
    = 822 ÷ 18 ≈ 45

3. 1 gallon of wax costs the same as 60 ÷ 2 = 30 bars of soap. Thus, 5 gallons of wax costs
    the same as (5)(30) = 150 bars of soap.

4. To average 280 sq.ft. for five days means a total of (5)(280) = 1400 sq.ft. for all five days.
    The number of square feet to be waxed on Friday = 1400 - (275+352+179+302) = 292

5. The acreage for buildings is 35 - 28 = 7. Then, 7/35 = 20%

6. (16)(3/4) = 12 quarts = 3 gallons. The amount of detergent, in ounces, is (2)(3) = 6. The
    amount of disinfectant is 1 oz.

7. One corn broom weighs 32 ÷ 12 = 2 2/3 lbs. ≈ 2 lbs. 11 oz.

8. Number of bulbs at the beginning of the year = (7)(12) + (14)(12) = 252. Number of bulbs
    replaced over an entire year = (5)(3)(12) = 180. The number of unused bulbs = 252 - 180
    = 72 = 6 dozen.

9. Total number of apartments = (4)(14)(10) = 560. The number of apartments with at least
    4 rooms = (.65)(560) = 364.

10. 30 ÷ 1 1/2 = 20. Then, (20)(30) = 600 flights of stairs

11. The number of windows washed by A, B, C were 30, 120, and 60. Their total is 210.

12. The two missing dimensions are 26 - 14 = 12 ft. and 33 - 9 = 24 ft. Perimeter = 9 + 12 +
    33 + 26 + 24 + 14 = 118 ft. Thus, total cost of fencing = (118)($7.50) = $885.00

13. $.625 = \dfrac{625}{1000} = \dfrac{5}{8}$

14. (12)(6)(4) = 288 cu.ft. Now, 1 cu.yd. = 27 cu.ft.; 288 cu.ft. is equivalent to 10 2/3 or about
    11 cu.yds.

15. 144 sq.in. = 1 sq.ft. The room measures (8 ft.)x(10 ft.) = 80 sq.ft. = 11,520 sq.in. Each tile
    measures (9)(9) = 81 sq.in. The number of tiles needed = 11,520 ÷ 81 = 142.2 or about
    142.

16. 20 ft. by 6 in. = (20 ft.)(1/2 ft.) = 10 sq.ft. Then, (10X.90) = $9.00

17. There will be 3 cuts in making 3 lengths of pipe, and these 3 cuts will use (3)(1/8) = 3/8
    in. of pipe. The amount of pipe remaining after the 3 pieces are removed = 36 - 12 1/4
    - 6 1/2 - 8 5/8 - 3/8 = 8 1/4 in.

18. The maintenance bond = (.10)($8,000,000) = $800,000

19. $(100)(200) = 20,000$ sq.ft. $= 20,000 \div 9 \approx 2222$ sq.yds. Then, $2222 \div 700 \approx 3.17$. Since a core must be taken for each 700 sq.yds. plus any left over fraction, 4 cores will be needed.

20. Six inches means $(6)(40) = 240$ ft. of actual length.

21. $(100$ ft.$)(110$ ft.$) = 11,000$ sq.ft. ≈ 1222 sq.yds. Then, since 1 acre $= 4840$ sq.yds., 1222 sq.yds. is equivalent to about 1/4 acre.

22. 1 in. $= 1/12$ ft. $\approx .08$ ft.

23. Area of $\triangle$ EFG $= (1/2)(8)(6) + (1/2)(4)(6) = 36$ sq.ft.

24. The amount to be retained $= (.05)(\$300,000) = \$15,000$

25. $(210)(30) = 6300$ sq.ft. Since 1 sq.yd. $= 9$ sq.ft., 6300 sq.ft. equals 700 sq.yds.

TEST 2

DIRECTIONS: Each question or incomplete statement is followed by several suggested answers or completions. Select the one that BEST answers the question or completes the statement. *PRINT THE LETTER OF THE CORRECT ANSWER IN THE SPACE AT THE RIGHT.*

1. The TOTAL length of four pieces of 2" pipe, whose lengths are 7'3 1/2", 4'2 3/16", 5'7 5/16", and 8'5 7/8", respectively, is   1.____

    A. 24'6 3/4"   B. 24'7 15/16"
    C. 25'5 13/16"   D. 25'6 7/8"

2. Under the same conditions, the group of pipes that gives the SAME flow as one 6" pipe is (neglecting friction) _____ pipes.   2.____

    A. 3 3"   B. 4 3"   C. 2 4"   D. 3 4"

3. A water storage tank measures 5' long, 4' wide, and 6' deep and is filled to the 5 1/2' mark with water.
If one cubic foot of water weighs 62 pounds, the number of pounds of water required to COMPLETELY fill the tank is   3.____

    A. 7,440   B. 6,200   C. 1,240   D. 620

4. A hot water line made of copper has a straight horizontal run of 150 feet and, when installed, is at a temperature of 45°F. In use, its temperature rises to 190°F.
If the coefficient of expansion for copper is 0.0000095" per foot per degree F, the total expansion, in inches, in the run of pipe is given by the product of 150 multiplied by 0.0000095 by   4.____

    A. 145   B. 145 x 12
    C. 145 divided by 12   D. 145 x 12 x 12

5. To dig a trench 3'0" wide, 50'0" long, and 5'6" deep, the total number of cubic yards of earth to be removed is MOST NEARLY   5.____

    A. 30   B. 90   C. 140   D. 825

6. If it costs $65 for 20 feet of subway rail, the cost of 150 feet of this rail will be   6.____

    A. $487.50   B. $512.00   C. $589.50   D. $650.00

7. The number of cubic feet of concrete it takes to fill a form 10 feet long, 3 feet wide, and 6 inches deep is   7.____

    A. 12   B. 15   C. 20   D. 180

8. The sum of 4 1/16, 51/4, 3 5/8, and 4 7/16 is   8.____

    A. 17 3/16   B. 17 1/4   C. 17 5/16   D. 17 3/8

9. If you earn $10.20 per hour and time and one-half for working over 40 hours, your gross salary for a week in which you worked 42 hours would be   9.____

    A. $408.00   B. $428.40   C. $438.60   D. $770.80

10. A drill bit, used to drill holes in track ties, has a diameter of 0.75 inches.   10._____
    When expressed as a fraction, the diameter of this drill bit is

    A. 1/4"   B. 3/8"   C. 1/2"   D. 3/4"

11. Three dozen shovels were purchased for use.   11._____
    If the shovels were used at the rate of nine a week, the number of weeks that the three
    dozen lasted was

    A. 3   B. 4   C. 9·   D. 12

12. Assume that you earn $20,000 per year.   12._____
    If twenty percent of your pay is deducted for taxes, social security, and pension, your
    weekly take-home pay will be MOST NEARLY

    A. $280   B. $308   C. $328   D. $344

13. If a measurement scaled from a drawing is one inch, and the scale of the drawing is 1/8   13._____
    inch to the foot, then the one inch measurement would represent an ACTUAL length of

    A. 8 feet   B. 2 feet
    C. 1/8 of a foot   D. 8 inches

14. Tiles 12" x 12" are used to lay a floor having the dimensions 10'0" x 12'0".   14._____
    The MINIMUM number of tiles needed to completely cover the floor is

    A. 60   B. 96   C. 120   D. 144

15. The volume of concrete in a strip of sidewalk 30 feet long by 4 feet wide by 3 inches thick   15._____
    is _____ cubic feet.

    A. 30   B. 120   C. 240   D. 360

16. To change a quantity of cubic feet into an equivalent quantity of cubic yards, _____ the   16._____
    quantity by _____.

    A. multiply; 9   B. divide; 9
    C. multiply; 27   D. divide; 27

17. If a pump can deliver 50 gallons of water per minute, then the time needed for this pump   17._____
    to empty an excavation containing 5,800 gallons of water is _____ hour(s) _____ min-
    utes.

    A. 2; 12   B. 1; 56   C. 1; 44   D. 1; 32

18. The sum of 3 1/6", 4 1/4", 3 5/8", and 5 7/16" is   18._____

    A. 15 9/16"   B. 16 1/8"   C. 16 23/48"   D. 16 3/4"

19. If a measurement scaled from a drawing is 2 inches, and the scale of the drawing is 1/8   19._____
    inch to the foot, then the two inch measurement would represent an ACTUAL length of

    A. 8 feet   B. 4 feet
    C. 1/4 of a foot   D. 16 feet

20. A room is 7'6" wide by 9'0" long with a ceiling height of 8'0". One gallon of flat paint will cover approximately 400 square feet of wall.
    The number of gallons of this paint required to paint the walls of this room, making no deductions for windows or doors, is MOST NEARLY

    A. 1/4　　　B. 1/2　　　C. 2/3　　　D. 1

20._____

21. The cost of a certain job is broken down as follows:

Materials	$3,750
Rental of equipment	1,200
Labor	3,150

    The percentage of the total cost of the job that can be charged to materials is MOST NEARLY

    A. 40%　　　B. 42%　　　C. 44%　　　D. 46%

21._____

22. By trial, it is found that by using two cubic feet of sand, a 5 cubic foot batch of concrete is produced. Using the same proportions, the amount of sand required to produce 2 cubic yards of concrete is MOST NEARLY _____ cubic feet.

    A. 20　　　B. 22　　　C. 24　　　D. 26

22._____

23. It takes 4 men 6 days to do a certain job.
    Working at the same speed, the number of days it will take 3 men to do this job is

    A. 7　　　B. 8　　　C. 9　　　D. 10

23._____

24. The cost of rawl plugs is $27.50 per gross. The cost of 2,448 rawl plugs is

    A. $467.50　　　B. $472.50　　　C. $477.50　　　D. $482.50

24._____

25. In a certain district, the area of a building may be no longer than 55% of the area of the lot on which it stands. On a rectangular lot 75 ft. by 125 ft., the maximum permissible area of building is, in square feet, MOST NEARLY

    A. 5,148　　　B. 5,152　　　C. 5,156　　　D. 5,160

25._____

KEY (CORRECT ANSWERS)

1.	D		11.	B
2.	B		12.	B
3.	D		13.	A
4.	A		14.	C
5.	A		15.	A
6.	A		16.	D
7.	B		17.	B
8.	D		18.	C
9.	C		19.	D
10.	D		20.	C

21.	D
22.	B
23.	B
24.	A
25.	C

SOLUTIONS TO PROBLEMS

1. $3\frac{1}{6}"+4\frac{1}{4}"+3\frac{5}{8}"+5\frac{7}{16}"+=3\frac{8}{48}"+4\frac{12}{48}"+3\frac{30}{48}"+5\frac{21}{48}"=15\frac{71}{48}"=16\frac{23}{48}"$

2. The flow of a 6" pipe is measured by the cross-sectional area. Since diameter = 6", radius = 3", and so area = 9π sq.in. A single 3" pipe would have a cross-sectional area of $(3/2)\pi$ sq.in. = 2.25π sq.in. Now, $9 \div / 2.25 = 4$. Thus, four 3" pipes is equivalent, in flow, to one 6" pipe.

3. (5x4x6) - (5x4x5 1/2) = 10. Then, (10)(62) = 620 pounds.

4. The total expansion = (150')(.0000095"/1 ft.)(190°-45°). So, the last factor is 145.

5. (3')(50')(5 1/2') = 825 cu.ft. Since 1 cu.yd. = 27 cu.ft., 825 cu.ft. cu.yds.

6. 150 ÷ 20 = 7.5. Then, (7.5)($65) = $487.50

7. (10')(3')(1/2') = 15 cu.ft.

8. $4\frac{1}{16}+5\frac{4}{16}+3\frac{10}{16}+4\frac{7}{16}=16\frac{22}{16}=17\frac{3}{8}$

9. Gross salary = ($10.20)(40) + ($15.30)(2) = $438.60

10. $75"=\frac{75}{100}"=\frac{3}{4}"$

11. 3 dozen = 36 shovels. Then, 36 ÷ 9 = 4 weeks

12. Since 20% is deducted, the take-home pay = ($20,000)(.80) = $16,000 for the year, which is $16,000 ÷ 52 ≈ $308 per week.

13. A scale drawing where 1/8" means an actual size of 1 ft. implies that a scale drawing of 1" means an actual size of (1')(8) = 8'

14. (10')(12') = 120 sq.ft. Since each tile is 1 sq.ft., a total of 120 tiles will be used.

15. (30')(4')(1/4') = 30 cu.ft.

16. To convert a given number of cubic feet into an equivalent number of cubic yards, divide by 27.

17. 5800 ÷ 50 = 116 min. = 1 hour 56 minutes

18. $3\frac{1}{6}"+4\frac{1}{4}"+3\frac{5}{8}"+5\frac{7}{16}"+=3\frac{8}{48}"+4\frac{12}{48}"+3\frac{30}{48}"+5\frac{21}{48}"=15\frac{71}{48}"=16\frac{23}{48}"$

19. 2 ÷ 1/8 = 16, so a 2" drawing represents an actual length of 16 feet.

20. The area of the 4 walls = 2(7 1/2')(8') + 2(9')(8') = 264 sq.ft. Then, 264 ÷ 400 = .66 or about 2/3 gallon of paint.

21. $3750 + $1200 + $3150 = $8100. Then, $3750/$8100 ≈ 46%

22. 2 cu.yds. ÷ 5 cu.ft. = 54 ÷ 5 = 10.8. Now, (10.8)(2 cu.ft.) ≈ 22 cu.ft. Note: 2 cu.yds. = 54 cu.ft.

23. (4)(6) = 24 man-days. Then, 24 ÷ 3 = 8 days

24. 2448 ÷ 144 = 17. Then, (17)($27.50) = $467.50

25. (75')(125') = 9375 sq.ft. The maximum area of the building = (.55)(9375 sq.ft.) * 5156 sq.ft.

TEST 3

DIRECTIONS: Each question or incomplete statement is followed by several suggested answers or completions. Select the one that BEST answers the question or completes the statement. *PRINT THE LETTER OF THE CORRECT ANSWER IN THE SPACE AT THE RIGHT.*

1. A steak weighed 2 pounds, 4 ounces.
   How much did it cost at $4.60 per pound?

   A. $7.80   B. $8.75   C. $9.90   D. $10.35

   1._____

2. twenty pints of water just fill a pail.
   the capacity of the pail, in gallons, is

   A. 2   B. 2 1/4   C. 2 1/2   D. 2 3/4

   2._____

3. The sum of 5/12 and 1/4 is

   A. 7/12   B. 2/3   C. 3/4   D. 5/6

   3._____

4. The volume of earth, in cubic yards, excavated from a trench 4'0" wide by 5'6" deep by 18'6" long is MOST NEARLY

   A. 14.7   B. 15.1   C. 15.5   D. 15.9

   4._____

5. 5/8 written as a decimal is

   A. 62.5   B. 6.25   C. .625   D. .0625

   5._____

6. The number of cubic feet in a cubic yard is

   A. 9   B. 12   C. 27   D. 36

   6._____

7. If it costs $16.20 to lay one square yard of asphalt, to lay a patch 15' by 15', it will cost MOST NEARLY

   A. $405.00   B. $3,645.00   C. $134.50   D. $243.00

   7._____

8. You are assigned thirty (30) asphalt workers to be divided into two crews so that one crew will have 2/3 as many men as the other.
   The number of men you would put into the SMALLER crew is

   A. 10   B. 12   C. 14   D. 20

   8._____

9. It takes 12 asphalt workers, working 6 hours a day, 5 days to complete a certain job.
   The number of days it will take 10 men, working 8 hours a day, to do the same job, assuming all work at the same rate, is

   A. 2 1/2   B. 3   C. 4 1/2   D. 6

   9._____

0. A street is laid to a 3% grade.
   This means that in 150 ft., the street grade will rise

   A. 4 1/2 inches   B. 45 inches
   C. 4 1/2 feet   D. 45 feet

   10._____

11. The sum of the following dimensions, 3 4/8, 4 1/8, 5 1/8, and 6 1/4, is   11.____

    A. 19   B. 19 1/8   C. 19 1/4   D. 19 1/2

12. A worker is paid $9.30 per hour.   12.____
If he works 8 hours each day on Monday, Tuesday, and Wednesday, 3 1/2 hours on
Thursday, and 3 hours on Friday, the TOTAL amount due him is

    A. $283.65   B. $289.15   C. $276.20   D. $285.35

13. The price of metal lath is $395.00 per 100 square yards. The cost of 527 square yards of   13.____
this lath is MOST NEARLY

    A. $2,076.50   B. $2,079.10   C. $2,081.70   D. $2,084.30

14. The total cost of applying 221 square yards of plaster board is $3,430.   14.____
The cost per square yard is MOST NEARLY

    A. $14.00   B. $14.50   C. $15.00   D. $15.50

15. In a three-coat plaster job, the scratch coat is 1/8 in. thick in front of the lath, the brown   15.____
coat is 3/16 in. thick, and the finish coat is 1/8 in. thick.
The TOTAL thickness of this plaster job, measured from the face of the lath, is

    A. 7/16"   B. 1/2"   C. 9/16"   D. 5/8"

16. If an asphalt worker earns $38,070 per year, his wages per month are MOST NEARLY   16.____

    A. $380.70   B. $735.00   C. $3,170.00   D. $3,807.00

17. The sum of 4 1/2 inches, 3 1/4 inches, and 7 1/2 inches is 1 foot _____ inches.   17.____

    A. 3   B. 3 1/4   C. 3 1/2   D. 4

18. The area of a rectangular asphalt patch, 9 ft. 3 in. by 6 ft. 9 in., is _____ square feet.   18.____

    A. 54   B. 54 1/4   C. 54 1/2   D. 62 7/16

19. The number of cubic feet in a cubic yard is   19.____

    A. 3   B. 9   C. 16   D. 27

20. A 450 ft. long street with a grade of 2% will have one end of the street higher than the   20.____
other end by _____ feet.

    A. 2   B. 44   C. 9   D. 20

21. If the drive wheel of a roller is 6 ft. in diameter and the tiller wheel is 4 ft. in diameter,   21.____
whenever the drive wheel makes a complete revolution on a straight pass, the tiller wheel
makes _____ revolution(s).

    A. 1   B. 1 1/4   C. 1 1/2   D. 2

22. A point on the centerline of a street is marked: Station 42 + 51. Another point on the cen-   22.____
terline 30 feet from the first is marked Station 42+81.
A third should be marked Station

    A. 12+51   B. 42+21   C. 45+51   D. 72+51

23. In twenty minutes, a truck moving with a speed of 30 miles an hour will cover a distance of _____ miles.

    A. 3   B. 5   C. 10   D. 30

23._____

24. The number of pounds in a ton is

    A. 500   B. 1,000   C. 2,000   D. 5,000

24._____

25. During his summer vacation, a boy earned $45.00 per day and saved 60% of his earnings.
If he worked 45 days, how much did he save during his vacation?

    A. $15.00   B. $18.00   C. $1,215.00   D. $22.50

25._____

KEY (CORRECT ANSWERS)

1.	D		11.	A
2.	C		12.	A
3.	B		13.	C
4.	B		14.	D
5.	C		15.	A
6.	C		16.	C
7.	A		17.	B
8.	B		18.	D
9.	C		19.	D
10.	C		20.	C

21.	C
22.	B
23.	C
24.	C
25.	C

SOLUTIONS TO PROBLEMS

1. ($4.60)(2 1/4 lbs.) = $10.35

2. 1 gallon = 8 pints, so 20 pints = 20/8 = 2 1/2 gallons

3. $\dfrac{5}{12}+\dfrac{1}{4}=\dfrac{5}{12}+\dfrac{3}{12}=\dfrac{8}{12}=\dfrac{2}{3}$

4. (4')(5 1/2')(18 1/2') = 407 cu.ft. Since 1 cu.yd. = 27 cu.ft., 407 cu.ft. $\approx$ 15.1 cu.yds.

5. 5/8=5 $\div$ 8.000 = .625

6. There are (3)(3)(3) =27 cu.ft. in a cu.yd.

7. (15')(15') = 225 sq.ft. = 25 sq.yds. Then, ($16.20)(25) = $405.00

8. Let 2x = size of smaller crew and 3x = size of larger crew. Then, 2x + 3x = 30. Solving, x = 6. Thus, the smaller crew consists of 12 workers.

9. (12)(6)(5) = 360 worker-days. Then, 360 $\div$ [(10)(8)] = 4 1/2 days

10. (.03)(150') = 4 1/2 ft.

11. $3\dfrac{4}{8}+4\dfrac{1}{8}+5\dfrac{1}{8}+6\dfrac{2}{8}=18\dfrac{8}{8}=19$

12. ($9.30)(8+8+8+3 1/2+3) = ($9.30)(30 1/2) = $283.65

13. The cost of 527 sq.yds. = (5.27)($395.00) = $2081.65 $\approx$ $2081.70

14. $3430 $\div$ 221 $\approx$ $15.50

15. $\dfrac{1}{8}"+\dfrac{3}{16}"+\dfrac{1}{8}"=\dfrac{2}{16}"+\dfrac{3}{16}"+\dfrac{2}{16}"=\dfrac{7}{16}"$

16. $38,070 $\div$ 12 = $3172.50 $\approx$ $3170.00 per month

17. 4 1/2" + 3 1/4" + 7 1/2" = 15 1/4" = 1 ft. 3 1/4 in.

18. 9 ft. 3 in. = 9 1/4 ft., 6 ft. 9 in. = 6 3/4 ft. Area = (9 1/4) (6 3/4) = 62 7/16 sq.ft.

19. A cubic yard = (3)(3)(3) = 27 cubic feet

20. (450')(.02) = 9 ft.

21. 6/4 = 1 1/2 revolutions

22. Station 42 + 51
    30 ft away would be 51 + 30 = 81 OR 51 - 30 = 21
    Station 42 + 81 or 42 + 21 (ANSWER: B)

23. 30 miles in 60 minutes means 10 miles in 20 minutes.

24. There are 2000 pounds in a ton.

25. ($45.00)(.60) = $27.00 savings per day. For 45 days, his savings is (45)($27.00) = $1215.00

———

Made in the USA
Middletown, DE
14 October 2023

40786953R00091